M000190846

PRAISE FOR *A LIFE WORTH LIVING*

A Life Worth Living is a book worth reading. Not only could I relate to many of the author's struggles, but also experienced a deep curiosity growing in me as I followed the stages of her transformational spiritual journey. Where would she take me next? This is not a book written with objectivity. It is the exact opposite. *A Life Worth Living* is written with a passion and fierceness that is the perfect antidote to any cool, above-it-all preaching about what happens when we commit ourselves to the path of yoga. I will gratefully carry the words of this Warrior-Princess-Seeker with me as I continue my own spiritual journey, feeling a little less lonely, a little less afraid, and a lot more inspired. Join us."

> — **Judith Hanson Lasater**, PhD, PT, international yoga teacher since 1971, author of 11 books, most recently *Teaching Yoga with Intention: The Essential Guide to Skillful Hands-on Assists and Verbal Communication*

Mellara's book dives deep into the passage of yoga and how we can use our practice (yoga), our breath, and our awareness to create more love and peace in our lives. I see so much of my own journey in Mellara's and suspect many others will relate to her journey as well.

> — **Mariel Hemingway**, actress and author of *Out Came the Sun*

A Life Worth Living is one woman's story of struggle, redemption, and deep learning. Mellara shows us how healing is possible through presence, devotion, and practical listening.

> — **Elena Brower**, author of *Being You* & other bestselling titles, and podcast host of *Practice You*

Mellara's love shines in her words of wisdom and practical Dharma teachings throughout *A Life Worth Living*. As she shares her journey with us, she sprinkles the path with supportive spiritual reminders that this life is precious and we can find inspiration and healing during even the most arduous moments. Keep this book by your side in these unsettling times!

> — **Núbia Teixeira**, author of *Yoga and the Art of Mudras*, Founder of Bhakti Nova School of Yoga, Dance & Reiki, and of "Nubia's Devotional Yoga Online School" on Patreon

A Life Worth Living is a spiritual memoir of awakening that is raw, brave, and universally touching. As she shares her engaging and often heart-wrenching journey, Mellara's spirit rises time and again to reach for the light. Her book inspires, gently guides, and humbly reveals her own struggles and commitment to a path that she has mastered through honesty, love, and perseverance. To read this book is to experience a shift, not through instruction necessarily, but through absorption of the transmission of energy that Mellara is offering page by page. This book is a powerful and effective meditation on love and resilience.

> — **Christine Burke**, author of *The Yoga Healer* and *The Power of Breath and Hand Yoga* and owner of Liberation Yoga Studio in Los Angeles

In this wonderful memoir and manual of yogic practice, Mellara brings us humbly and deftly into her experience, and in so doing into our own—and we come out the other end changed for the better. Mellara's love, light, and beauty can be felt in every word.

— **Melanie Salvatore-August**, author of *Fierce Kindness* and *Yoga to Support Immunity*

A Life Worth Living:

A Journey of Self-Discovery Through Mindfulness, Yoga, and Living in Awareness

Mellara Gold

Copyright © 2021 by Mellara Gold
ISBN: 978-1950186358

All rights reserved. No part of this publication may be repro-
duced or transmitted in any form or by any means, mechanical or
electronic, including photocopying and recording, or by any information storage and retrieval system, without permission in
writing from the author and/or publisher.

All permissions are held by the author, who releases the publisher
from all liability.

Cover photo by Teo Tarras, "Woman with yoga pose in Bud-
    dhist temple." Image used under license from Shutter-
    stock.com
Author photo on back cover, copyright © Vessa Ventz
Author photo on page 249, copyright © In Her Image Photog-
    raphy
Cover design copyright © Lisa Carta Carta Design, 2021

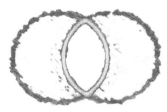

MANDORLA BOOKS
WWW.MANDORLABOOKS.COM

Author's Note

The contents of this book are for informational and inspirational purposes only and are not a substitute for professional therapeutic, pastoral, or medical advice, diagnosis, or treatment. Any application of the material in the following pages is at the reader's discretion and is their sole responsibility. Neither the author nor the publisher is responsible for any adverse effects resulting from the use or reliance on any information contained in this book.

All of the stories in this book are true, but the names of some individuals have been changed.

Cultivating understanding and compassion
for oneself and others
through living in awareness

Practicing the teachings
inspired by Channa Dassanayaka
has been transformational for me

Table of Contents

Invocation

by Channa Dassanayaka

❧

I was born in Sri Lanka and raised a Buddhist. As a young man, I practiced in a Buddhist monastery, then to Australia, where I live today and offer teachings we call Uniting Awareness. It is a practice of compassion and presence, interweaving elements of Eastern spirituality, yoga asanas, and psychological insight.

In the Buddhist tradition, at the beginning of a ceremony, we put flowers on the altar, light a candle, place burning incense in a bowl of finely filtered ash, and ring the temple gong. To introduce Mellara's book, I shall do the same.

The fragrance of the flowers represents innocence, the many dreams we thought would bring us happiness. Placing flowers on the shrine, we realize the body and image we believed ourselves to be are not who we are. Flowers wilt over time, and watching them, we observe impermanence—that body, image, and all things will sooner or later return to the earth. We've traveled far from our original innocence, and witnessing impermanence helps us remember our life's purpose beyond image and even body. May we realize who we truly are.

The candle represents the longing to know ourselves, not just through the intellect, but to see and feel what is really inside. This is beyond knowledge, free of gender and any other identity. We can only know this wisdom from within. In light, darkness evaporates and we see things as they are. The light of the candle signifies truly knowing ourselves and others.

Burning incense perfumes all of nature, helping us reconnect with the fragrance of our innermost innocence. As I ring the bell and offer sound, I experience myself as a series of vibrations without a story. When I reach this level of understanding, I can feel the practice in my heart and allow myself to awaken to the reality of things as they are. May all beings awaken to their true selves.

Introduction

"Sometimes being lost is the best way to find yourself."
— L. J. Vanier, *Ether: Into the Nemesis*

When I was a young girl growing up in Australia in the 1980s, feeling lost did not feel good. As a woman living now in the United States, it still doesn't feel good, but I've learned through hardship the truth of L. J. Vanier's line, that sometimes being lost is the best way, or even the only way, to find oneself.

Sometimes when I'm feeling this way now, I'll drop into child's pose for a few minutes. If you are a yoga student, you might know this position as the place where you finally get a rest and can reflect on what your practice might be trying to teach you. The quietness in the room, your eyes closed, and the hum of your breath facilitate reading the barometer of your soul's understanding for that moment.

I'm a yoga teacher, yet above anything else what I love most is being a student of this ancient practice. Growing up, I had no intention of being a yoga teacher. It was slow, boring, and certainly not exciting enough for my teenaged self. Yoga came to me when I was living in Los Angeles trying to support myself with odd jobs like waitressing, stand-in actress, apartment manager, and anything else that could further my dream of becoming a Hollywood actress. And I was in pain.

Quite honesty I was a mess. I was living alone in the US with no support system that felt reliable. Outwardly I portrayed myself as having self-worth, so you may not have noticed that I was drowning in self-pity half the time. I would play dumb when I needed to and play smart to get my way, and everything in the middle that I needed to do to survive. Basically, whatever you needed me to be, I was your gal. Above anything else I had to have folks love me, because I didn't love or accept myself enough to compromise. I had much to work on and yearned to develop an inner strength and authenticity that included all aspects of life. But I didn't know this until I got closer to forty and moved back to Australia with my husband and two children. In my younger years all I knew is that I needed relief from the pain I was feeling and fast! Not unlike a lot of folks who practice postural yoga, I was on the mat to find relief from the back pain that I was experiencing, and later I became a teacher of it.

At seventeen I was diagnosed with five bulging discs, and I knew I had to find a way to help heal myself. This was the external circumstance that brought me to yoga. Internally, I know now, I wasn't settled within until I began to include the teachings of yoga and meditation into my whole life. Only then did I begin to heal my whole self, my body, mind, and spirit. This is the journey toward a life worth living that I've come to share with you in this book.

This book is not here to convince you to practice yoga or be a teacher of it, or to beat yourself up over all the good things that you could be doing for yourself that you're not, like meditating or joining an intentional community such as the one I'll describe in this book—though perhaps you're already doing all of these things too, and know their value. No, it's a book to help support us where we are in life no matter if we have yet to try yoga or are deep in the practice. It is a book to help support us in becoming quieter within so we can awaken to the mystery of this human realm. All of us have unfinished business when it comes to our healing, but that doesn't mean we are not already enough. We are enough, and this book and these teachings are here to help us remember that. Through a practice of self-discovery, we can learn to love in the presence of pain, and to stay centered in the midst of being lost.

We all have something that reminds us of when we're not

living in balance, and for me it has been back pain. I explore this chronic pain and my desire for love and self-acceptance during the time when dis-ease still had the upper hand. In LA, I became a teen bride and a US citizen. With unbearable back pain and a chronic feeling of worthlessness, I was angry at life and God and completely disconnected from myself. It was then that I tried to quell the pain by ending my life with an overdose of pills in a hot bath. Fortunately, as I woke up in an LA hospital, a psychiatrist talked me through what had happened and kept me under observation for four more days to be sure I didn't hurt myself again. Though this was well over two decades ago, writing about it in this book still evokes the frightening nature of that time when I was so lost that I wanted to die.

As I write this introduction, I am beginning to feel exposed, vulnerable, tummy bloated, and my heart beating faster with my shoulders up just a little closer to my ears than I would like them to be. This happened a lot during the writing of this book and all stages of the publication process. What I didn't realize would happen happens again and again—all of my unresolved shit rises up to the surface for yet another close up. As I write this, I've signed with my publisher and am only months away from publishing this book you have in your hands. Perhaps you know the feeling when you think you have finally healed something, and then BAM! The universe brings in just the right person, situation, or in my case, book to write and publish that helps us grow and understand ourselves a bit more. I feel like our healing looks like the infinity symbol, kind of like one step/loop forward, two steps back, or at times five steps forward and only one step back.

Sometimes during this process I've asked myself, why can't I just live my life and not write these stories from my life to ultimately share with you? Why do I do it with such purpose and determination, and yet at the same time feel so bloody scared? I think it all goes back to healing. Something happens to us when we get our stories out from inside us and into the world. We feel cracked wide open, perhaps lighter, and maybe we might even get to the place where we no longer feel like we have to hide behind them, identify with them, or feel ashamed of them. At least this is part of the "why" for me.

Still, even now, my mind is moving from one place to another like a monkey in a tree while my ego is trying to protect me. Questions come flooding into my mind like:

Who do you think you are, no one wants to read your story! You are not famous, and you are not at the end of a long life where you might have a ton of wisdom to impart.

If not watched, our mind can wreak havoc on our self-esteem. But in the end, I know that playing small, from the mind's perspective, keeps us safe. But it also keeps us stuck and non-creative with a soul yearning to finally be asked out to the dance.

Still, I'm human, which means there's sometimes a gap between what I know and what I experience. The monkey rattles the branches with other intrusive questions and thoughts like:

You have managed to create a new life for yourself so different from the dysfunction you were born in to. So, it's better to just leave the past in the past and lock away the key!

You are betraying your family of origin who in the end were just doing their best. Who are you to bring it all out on the table and potentially shame them like this?

You have children and the audience is watching.

You will be judged.

And the biggest one of all:

You will be found out, made unlovable!

This is probably my greatest fear. Still, I cannot shake this feeling that my soul wants me to get it all out, heal more completely, and bring the underbelly of the deepest parts of me and our common humanity to the surface.

Vulnerability certainly lives in my underbelly, and most likely in yours as well, which is why I share this part of my process of bringing this book to you. In 2016, I realized just how vulnerable publication would be. I had completed the first draft of this book, and found an incredible editor to polish it up. I remember clearly what I said to him, with sweaty palms and my voice shaking: "If I give you the whole manuscript to read, to me it is like I'm standing naked in front of a stranger." Afterwards I felt so embarrassed that I even said that, but it was, and remains true.

And yet here I am, still standing. Now, writing these final words in 2021, I understand that I have come so far. I think sometimes we have to acknowledge how far we have come in our healing because if we don't, we might miss the extra sauce that is waiting for us on the other side of the lessons.

My heart knows that it's important to share my ugly, sometimes raw and messy truth with you. That using our voice for change is one of the best things any of us can do to help make our world the place we would like to live in. I'm not sharing my stories for you to feel sorry for me—trust me, I've done enough of that to fill up many lifetimes of sorrow. No, I'm sharing them and some wisdom I've gathered along the way because I know I'm not the only one who has felt lost, untrusting, and unworthy. If only more of us could bring our stories to the surface for healing. While we bring them out, we don't have to live alone with them and any shame surrounding them. We don't have to be alone with our unstable childhood environment that molded us, feeling deprived, anxious, and depressed. Once childhood is over, there may be no going back, but through what I call in this book "living in awareness," we can still learn to thrive.

I carry many hopes for you who are reading these pages. I hope you may observe your own greatest superpower that arose from a survival strategy that you may have developed when you were little. I hope you'll see that having an authentic relationship with your inner life draws you toward your unique calling and lets you love and be loved. I hope you'll see what's already working in your life, to see that you've been on the right track even if at times you took the most seemingly massive turn away from who you really are, or a series of smaller turns that had you spinning and feeling lost.

My life is a story of turns both small and massive. After ten years in Hollywood, two failed marriages, a bankruptcy, a suicide attempt, and nowhere to turn, I somehow listened to my inner guidance and went back to live in Australia in an attempt to understand the masculine. Growing up, I only knew neglect, abuse, and how untrustworthy my dad and mum were. My dad was a drug dealer on the Gold Coast, in and out of jail, and I never had the chance to understand him or why things were the way they were. Like many children in broken homes, I blamed myself and never thought I was enough.

Years later I met the man of my dreams and finally married well. My husband to this day meets me where I am at and personifies the nurturance and trustworthiness I didn't receive as a child. But I almost sabotaged our relationship even with the white picket fence and two beautiful children. Perhaps it was because life with someone kind and normal just didn't feel normal to me. Without the familiar drama, life just didn't feel right.

Well, the universe had other ideas, and I received an intervention of great proportions, a calling from the deepest part of who I am. Enter Channa Dassanayaka, a spiritual guru from the other side of the planet from where I was living at the time. Channa doesn't like to be called a guru, yet to me he meets every part of the definition. A guru is someone who guides the spiritual progress of their students, and as he did, I wrote it all down—the good, bad, and indifferent right inside this book you hold.

This isn't a story about how finding a guru or teacher is the only way toward a better understanding of ourselves, or how a magical other can take our worries and cares away. If someone says this to us and we think it's true, we're in danger of living someone else's life. To paraphrase Mary Oliver, we have one wild and precious life which is ours and ours alone.

Still, there is this saying: when the student is ready, the teacher will appear. I believe in the power of teachers, whether they are gurus, community leaders, therapists, life coaches, authors, public figures, podcasters, social activists, historical figures, or, closer to home, our family, our spouses, our friends, our children, even our animal companions and the beauty of nature around us. In the middle parts of this book, Channa appeared just when I needed him, and I was devoted to him, but you'll read about my other teachers as well—in the first part of this book, they were my parents and grandparents and the natural beauty of my native Australia, and in the last part, my beloved husband and children play a major role, along with some dear friends. All of them played a role in bringing me to this place where I can honestly say I have a life worth living.

And maybe, too, when the student is ready, the teacher will disappear. By this I mean that the teachings will remain, but the teacher may fade into the background as we step into the fore-ground of our own lives. For a period of time that I describe in this book, you'll see that I was thoroughly devoted to Channa. In his presence, I was able to see myself more clearly and heal so many of my wounds. As this stage of my journey comes to a close, I remain so grateful to Channa, but I wouldn't consider myself a devotee to him as my teacher any longer—he is, after all, just another spirit having a human experience, with feet of clay like us all—but through his teachings, I am now a devotee to love and to life itself, and I own my own light.

I believe that the way that teaching and healing come to us is much less important than the fact that teaching and healing come at all. And I've learned, and I'll show you this in the book, that there are some necessary preconditions to healing. True healing happens when we listen to ourselves; when we trust in the process; and when we participate with the universe, working with the conditions around us, to co-create a life worth living.

∽

As I share my healing journey with you, which of course is never complete, I imagine that it might make you reflect upon your own healing, to acknowledge both how far you have come in your own journey, but also, the ways in which it is not complete either. So, I offer this: If you feel triggered throughout the reading of this book, if things come up for you, I invite you to acknowledge your feelings and be with yourself so you can process these feelings.

One way to do so is to be as present as you can with yourself as you dive into these pages. Notice your body sensations, and whether you become hot or cold or experience other physical changes when reading different parts of the book. Through a non-judgmental and compassionate eye, I invite you to take note of where in your body your feelings are arising. Through my own experience staying present with wounds as they arise, I have come to the conclusion that if I am *feeling* my wounds, then I am *not* my wounds. My wounds are present, but they are not me; they are passing through me, but they do not define me or make me who I am.

I've learned over time to witness my frightened little child and let her know that she's safe staying within and that I am no longer that little one who didn't have any agency. So, if your frightened little child appears while you're reading this book, I reach out my hand to them. Together we can cheer each other on while venturing into the basement of what it means to be human, to be a spirit having this wild and crazy human experience.

Going into the basement is difficult work. It can be dark there, and full of shadows. We may meet disowned parts of ourselves, fearful parts, vulnerable parts, parts we may not love. And yet, deep inner work is the true meeting with ourselves—*all parts of ourself*—a true communion with our light and with our shadow. We do this deep inner work not from a place of self-judgment, but rather, from a place of self-acceptance. The reward of this work is living authentically as a more whole and complete human being. Now that's a life worth living!

I've found that self-acceptance means I must love all of myself, *all of my selves*, and not just the sweet parts that my outer world likes to acknowledge the most. At the heart of everything, I am a mother to Leela, Charlie, Rosie our pup, and little Mellara, who at times needs the same reassurance that I give my family. They are my priorities, along with my husband Mike with whom I am dedicated to live, love and laugh my way through all life's ups and downs.

I am also an author. Not an authority, but an author, a woman who has been writing my healing journey for years now, with the fervent hope that it will find readers like you, and offer you hope, encouragement, companionship, and maybe a little inspiration on your journey toward your most authentic, whole, and loving self. Today I can say that I wholeheartedly believe in myself, and I know that a life worth living is not only possible, but available to me, available to you, right here, right now.

In light and love,
Mellara Gold

PART ONE

Early Mud Years

On a retreat in Bali, I sat alongside the lotus pond and looked at the blooming flowers. It was clear in my mind's eye that the mud represented my early life and that it's possible to emerge from the mud into an exquisite flower. In fact, flower and mud have never been separated from each other, or from their source.

CHAPTER ONE

The Gold Coast

In order for you to understand my healing journey, I need to take you all the way back to my birth and my early childhood, where the wounding began for me, and most likely, where it began for you as well.

I grew up in Queensland, Australia, with 4,000 miles of shoreline that includes the world-famous Gold and Sunshine Coasts, and offshore, the Great Barrier Reef. My dad wasn't living with us before I was born, and was in and out of prison for supplying drugs to the lost souls of the Gold Coast. He came back and then left, over and over again, and around the time I was ten months old, my mum and dad got married.

It was 1975, and my parents had been dating for four years when they found out they were pregnant. My mum was just twenty and my dad twenty-one, and they didn't choose to have a baby, and probably wouldn't have chosen to marry if they hadn't gotten pregnant with me. I got the message clearly and repeatedly that I wasn't wanted. I recall my mum saying that she wished that someone would have taken her aside to help her deal with the pain and anger that she was feeling. One day, my dad told me that Mum was planning to sell me to the Mafia, as there was a high premium on blue-eyed, blond-haired babies. I don't know if that was true—it might have been—or if he was teasing, but it added to the burden of feeling unwanted. Mum tried to assure me, "At least I didn't give you up for adoption," which is what young unwed mothers did in those days. I wasn't starving or homeless or without clothes or a warm bed, but as a sensitive child, I was deeply affected by Dad's rage and neglect and Mum's mood swings.

I was very little, maybe three or four, when my father would threaten me with his belt, taking it off quickly, raising it in the air, and slamming it down on the table if I didn't eat all my dinner. I still occasionally have flashbacks when someone takes off their belt, but it doesn't have the same hold on me as it once did. Dad's abuse was primarily threats and yelling rather than direct physical harm, but it was scary, and mostly I just did whatever he said. One time at my mum's parents' house when I was about six, Dad was yelling so hard at me to get me to swallow a vitamin, and I was crying saying that I didn't know how. My grandfather stepped in and said, "Craig, that's enough. She can't do it, just leave it now." He did stop, but it was kind of like he was in a trance, acting out what had been done to him when he was little. And sometimes my dad would yell at me to go out in the big surf with him, saying it was safe. Nothing feels safe when you're being yelled at. He'd throw the surfboard over a wave and say, "See, the board comes back, and so will you."

What was saddest to me was what he *didn't* do. He never went to a school play to watch me act. He never read to me or looked at my report cards or picked me up at school to take me somewhere fun. His absence, I think, was the most damaging. From the beginning of my birth Dad would come and go from the places that we lived. He had other places to live like his mother's apartment and friends' couches. Even though we usually lived close by and could have done these things, I just wasn't on his radar, so I always thought something must be wrong with me. I just wanted him to love me like my friends' daddies did, and felt I was never enough.

I looked up highly to my mum even though she could be dismissive and mean to me. I thought she was the most beautiful woman in the world, certainly much more prettier than me. I knew I was pretty, but to me my mum was a goddess. When I would watch her roll a joint with the Tally-Ho brand papers and lick the paper to seal it, she did it with such grace and style, kind of like a scene out of an old Hollywood movie. As a kid I thought she was so smart and knew everything—she was cool, sometimes edgy, and did whatever the hell she wanted. She was a true artist acting out every bit of the shadow side of that role, both troubled and unpredictable. If she got mad about something, you wouldn't want to mess with my mum. There was a time at the roller rink when I was about eleven when some kid had stolen my purse and wouldn't give it back to me. I called Mum from the telephone at the rink and she asked if the boy was still there and I said yes, and she came marching in and asked me where the boy was without a hello and went right up to the teenaged boy's face demanding that he return what was mine. That boy knew not to mess her and as he brought it out from his side, she snapped it so fast out of his hands and quickly gave it to me. The boy seemed worried about what might happen next and I was in shock that she did this for me. I remember looking at her that day in awe at her strength, but also feeling some intense embarrassment and shame. In that moment, she spoke with such authority and was defending me, yet at other times she wasn't able to protect me from the same rage that she felt inside and took out on me.

My mum bullied me in different ways; her main weapon was invalidation. I can still sometimes hear her voice in my head snarling, "You with your perfect blonde hair, who do you think you are?" Probably she would say things like this as an attempt to shrink me down to size when she felt bad about herself and had run out of dope to smoke to numb her pain. So I learned at a young age to play small. "You are your father's daughter, selfish and lacking any kind of self-reflection," she would say. Then a pattern of feeling guilty would occur and she would lick her wounds, looking for validation. Sometimes when she got like this, my younger brother and I would try to reassure her that she was loved by us and that she was a good mother, but she didn't seem to listen. Unfortunately though, this roller-coaster ride seemed to go on forever, and she would dismiss my feelings and undermine my worth at every opportunity. She blamed me for the ways life had let her down, and I simply longed for both my parents' acceptance. Mum was nurturing when I got sick, but her ability to manipulate and destabilize me the rest of the time is something that as an adult, I'm still finding my way through.

After decades of processing all of this, my mum finally apologized for not being fully up to the task of being a mum, and for the drama surrounding my early life. At first I felt numb—I don't think I was able to really receive and process what she was saying. And after all those years of feeling belittled as a child, all she really wanted was to show kindness. Was this really my mum and was she even telling me the truth? I wondered. Did she really feel sorry and why all of a sudden now? Why didn't she say something like this years ago when I needed her the most?

Just a week or so after receiving her apology I was in Target with my twelve-year-old son Charlie, and my perception was that he didn't say "excuse me" before he barged his way through the small opening between a man and another checkout, kind of like I've seen him do when he plays basketball and he is making his way to the hoop. The man didn't seem too fazed and kept typing on his phone while letting me know not to worry about it. I still asked Charlie to apologize. Charlie was visibly embarrassed to be put on the spot, and his ears and forehead began to change to a reddish tone. When we got into the car, he told me he did say excuse me, and that I had it all wrong, it's just that nobody could hear him underneath the face mask he was wearing because of the pandemic. I did think for a moment that could be true and didn't know why I couldn't just let this one be and believe him fully, especially since we were both so tired after a long day and now angry with each other.

That night as I tucked Charlie into bed I apologized for not believing him, but still wondered what that was all about. It appeared to be about Charlie, but I felt that there was more to uncover there. What was my learning in all of this? And why did I make it into such a big deal and become so unsettled and upset? My go-to when this kind of thing happens is to be hard on myself and beat myself up, only making things worse. I've gotten better with this throughout the years, and yet like any of us, I am still a work in progress. I've also noticed that when I get like this, something is usually trying to make its way up to the surface of my awareness for healing, like something is being uncovered, some kind of realization that I just need to trust in myself and the process.

The next day as I was making the bed and the kids were already at school I received an overwhelming sensation that permeated through my whole body. A sudden flush of energy that I could only describe as deep sorrow mixed with compassion enveloped me. It was overwhelming and I began to cry, tears flooding down my face. My husband came in from the other room, and worriedly asked me what happened and if I was okay. With slow sobbing floods of tears pouring down my face, I told him that my pain of not believing Charlie was uber present and somehow through that pain I feel my mum's deep pain of me not believing in her pain. When things like this happen to me I usually like to be alone, but my husband has learned to hold space for me and just allow me my moment to be as I am. I don't know what happened to me that morning, but my relationship with my mum felt so much more resolved and a profound sense of peace and forgiveness for myself and my mother suddenly became my new normal. Perhaps I slipped into her shoes for a little bit and through the tears we share, I could somehow feel and see myself in hers; two individual human beings on a similar journey of self-love and acceptance.

Finally, I'm able to appreciate my mum's many colors and my own beautiful hues as well. I love my mum and I know that she loves me. She made many sacrifices so my brother and I could have some of what we needed as kids. She did the best she could to parent us, and I see now that the hole in my heart can only be healed by learning to love myself.

Refuge

Both of my parents loved to surf, and I have the fondest memories of walking with them along pure white-sand beaches to find the best waves, usually in Kirra or Burleigh Heads. I've always felt at home with the smell of sea air and the gentle caress of the sun's rays—and especially the healing balm of being inside the miraculous, warm Aussie waves that I was blessed to encounter at a young age.

We moved a lot, mostly to beautiful places—rainforests and beaches—and I spent a lot of my early years outdoors, which was a refuge to me. But moving so much, my deepest wish was to *belong*—first with my family, then my friends' families, and eventually the drama class at school, where I loved acting, singing, and being on stage. I longed to feel safe and loved, and I never let anyone know how much I was hurting inside. As a caregiver, I just focused on helping others.

My maternal grandparents were reasonably healthy role models, and they were also a refuge. Throughout my childhood we never lived more than a two-hour drive away from them. My grandma—I called her Mammiee—loved her home and garden, and enjoyed sipping tea on the patio. For decades she played the church piano and organ. On Saturday nights, we five grandkids would gather with our parents at Mammiee's to sing. Mum would play the flute, Grandma would play the piano while her sister Anne played the organ (or vice versa), and her brother Jimmy would sing so beautifully it reminded us of Frank Sinatra. We all knew the words to every song from Australian folk to big-band classics. There was always lots of food and good cheer. Still, Mum was usually glum, probably because she wasn't able to self-medicate with pot because they might find out, and by the end of the evening she and her brother Matthew would be fighting about something.

Christmas gatherings at my grandparents' were huge. Even in the blazing Aussie summer, we'd devour hot roast lamb, turkey, ham with all the fixings, and Christmas pudding as if we were in

England. Flies and hot humid nights were all part of our gatherings. After dinner, the adults would sit outside and drink, and we kids would run around the house and chase each other till we dropped.

My grandfather—I called him Papa—loved nature and took us camping all the time. I enjoyed watching him set up camp and teach us the ways of the bush. At home he'd water his garden every day, and I still love the smell of freshly cut grass, as it reminds me of Papa's beloved garden. He was also a big fan of Australiana, especially Aussie history. Papa was warm to me, and it was no secret that I was his favorite grandchild. My mum resented the attention on me and not my brother. The attention may have been because I was with my grandparents a lot more growing up than my brother ever was, especially since we are almost ten years apart in age and my mother eventually moved with my brother far enough away from my grandparents once I had left home.

My grandpa and I had a bond as big as the sky and whenever he noticed I was sad about something he would take me out for ice cream or get me something from the take-away shop. My grandma was my everything too. I remember when I lived with them we had a ritual—we would watch the news together and I would lay stretched out lengthways on the couch with my grandma on one side and my papa on the other. I was like an open sandwich in the middle and we would have this on-going joke that Mammiee would always get my head and Papa my stinky feet. I don't think my feet were ever that stinky but there is usually a bit of truth in every joke, and we would play out the same joke and laugh so hard every single night. Those were beautiful moments.

One time at my grandparents' home on the Sunshine Coast, I noticed a brochure on Papa's side table that said, "Win a luxury dream home with the Mater Prize Home lottery," and I began jumping up and down uncontrollably. I told him we were going to win and that he *had* to buy a ticket immediately. Papa had retired at age fifty from Trans Australia Airlines and had lots of time on his hands. He told me the draw for the lottery closed at

5 p.m. and we'd better get to town right away if we wanted to buy the ticket. I said—quite emphatically—"Let's go!" and off we went. We got to the ticket place on time and he *won* the house! Mammiee was overjoyed, and they moved in straight away. They sold their modest home in Bli Bli, a rural town in the Sunshine Coast region, for about $30,000. With the money they upgraded their camping gear, Mammiee got that new piano and organ that she had always dreamt of and everyone seemed overjoyed. Their new home was located in the Logan area in Shailer Park, a few miles outside of Brisbane between city, surf, and bay. This was in 1980, and a $200,000 home was, to me, a palace! We were in the local papers and all the news.

The Mater Prize home was a place of refuge for our whole family. I'd wake up early there, greet Papa, and together we'd prepare breakfast for Mammiee, usually two Weetabixes (a British cereal like Shredded Wheat), honey, milk, and a banana. After the table was set, Mammiee and I would cuddle in bed and recite the "Our Father" together. She told me to remember this prayer above all. Just above her bed, Mammiee had the famous painting of Jesus with his robe open revealing his sacred heart. I couldn't take my eyes off of it, mystified by a heart so open and exposed. Once Mammiee was up she would come downstairs with me for breakfast and there would be this on-going joke where I would grab the plastic banana that came with the winning of the house. And I would replace my papa's real banana with the plastic one. It doesn't seem like the biggest and funniest joke of all time, but boy, we would laugh so hard while Papa would carry on trying to peel the plastic banana like a scene in a movie. As a child these moments of bonding and laughing with them became a foundation for what I imagined family life might be like when I became old enough to have a family of my own.

As the morning light flooded through the stained-glass windows in the vaulted ceilings, I had a lot to dream about and hope for in life. Winning this house showed me that the world can change in a heartbeat. I knew it had been granted by God's grace. My grandparents lived to be nearly 100 and spent the rest of their lives there.

"All That Stuff"

When I was five, Mammiee offered to pay for my education if I attended Catholic school, and so I did for most of grade one. My parents weren't religious, perhaps more on the spiritual side than anything else, and my mum resented the Catholic Church. Growing up Mum and her brothers would go to church on Sundays and also went to Catholic school. I remember my mum being given some kind of ultimatum from her parents, mostly her mother, who had the strongest connection to her beloved religion. I think it went down something like this: "We will take care of Mellara only if she attends Catholic school." The nuns were strict, and I got into trouble for the littlest things. One day I asked Anne, the girl next to me, if I could borrow her eraser, and Sister Mary hit me with a ruler so hard my hand ended up with welts. Despite it all, I felt a sense of pride being in Catholic school and wearing the uniform. Maybe it was the love I had for Mammiee or perhaps another attempt to belong to *something*. I so wanted to be normal, or special, or anything other than feel as terrible as I did. I never thought about what I wanted or needed, only others, both at school and at home. But invariably I'd say the wrong thing, and hard as I tried, I never won the other kids over. It didn't help that one morning I threw up in the middle of the busy outside hallway in front of everyone. Kids stopping to look while some boy yelled out, "Yuck, look at her, isn't her name Malaria like the disease?" It was humiliating, and I guess I had a twenty-four-hour bug, and went home shortly after. But that set the tone for me, and the feeling of belonging felt way too far out of my reach. So instead of being with the other kids during breaks, I'd walk around the school grounds collecting trash, for which I received a service pin.

Just a few months before first grade and until halfway through that year, my parents and I lived in an old house on a Brahman bull farm outside the Gold Coast. Mum was introduced to horses as a young girl and was an experienced rider. I love looking at her childhood photos in the 1960s riding horses on the beach. Papa worked hard to provide for his three children, Mum being the youngest. It looked like an ideal childhood, but it wasn't. Throughout her childhood, I later learned, she was abused by a family member. She held it all in and managed to carry her love for horses into adulthood. After the win of the house Papa bought her a horse that she named Shandy, and in exchange for boarding on the farm, she helped Jon, the owner, look after his bulls.

My dad was with us a lot more during this time and they both were heavily into the drug scene. Weed and mushrooms at first and cocaine shortly followed as the 80's latest high found its way into Australia and my home. Strange visitors would show up at all hours of the day and night. Drug paraphernalia was out in the open, like seeds from the marijuana plant, half-torn Tally-Ho papers, and makeshift joint filters that were made out of cardboard. I thought that was normal, but not so normal that I would speak of it at school, I think because I had overheard my grandparents speaking badly about my dad and saying that he needed to stop doing "all that stuff." Like it was only my dad's fault when clearly it was both of them. One night, my dad was badly beaten, his face covered with purple and red bruises. Mum told me he had narc'd on somebody to get less jail time. To me, it was just Dad being Dad. Sometimes I would wonder why my mum would put up with all of that, but she was broken and traumatized after all the years of being abused and no one believing in her. I think she mostly turned a blind eye to my dad and all his drama because she was on her own similar journey to quell the pain. In the end I feel it was kind of a choiceless choice for my mum as she was finding the temporary relief that she so desperately needed, and I just happened to be in the middle of it all.

As a child, my dad was neglected and mistreated too, and as a result would take out the pain of his upbringing on me. I still remember him telling me that his mother would take him to her bed and hit him over and over again with the strap. Dad would take off his belt and hit me with it too, repeating the generational cycle of abuse. And when he did this I never gave in, because as sensitive as I was, I also had a stubborn streak. I yearned for his love and attention and hated him for doing this while wishing so badly for a brother or a sister to stand with me against this tyrant. While I yearned for a sibling to help me fight against this meanie, I also wanted someone to love. I kind of lost all hope that I would have a sibling because he didn't arrive until I was nearly ten years old. But when he did it was so worth the wait and we continue to have a strong bond today.

While living on the farm I experienced a lot of nightmares. In one recurring dream, demons carried me out of our house and held me down so I couldn't move. Grant Kenny, the great Aussie surfer, would then save me. When I woke up after this and other scary dreams, I'd turn the TV on to *Thunderbirds*, a British sci-fi program about a secret organization that saved people's lives. For certain important missions, they brought in Lady Penelope Creighton-Ward, who drove around in a Rolls-Royce. I imagined myself as Lady Penelope. Dad and Mum were asleep in the next room. I thought I had the volume low enough, but sometimes Dad would come running out, yelling and waving his arms, and he'd grab my little five-year-old arms and hit me over and over on my bottom.

Even at five years old, I showed signs of stress. I had urinary tract infections, and the doctors couldn't figure out why. They asked Mum if I was being molested. Asking that question brought more tension between my parents, as my mum thought I might have been sexually abused by my dad. Fortunately, this wasn't the case, but the yelling and physical fighting between them and toward me was beyond toxic.

I would later learn that indeed, urinary tract infections can be a result of anxiety. The sacral chakra pertains to the kidneys, which filter how we relate to those closest to us, what we hold onto and what we let go of, and being sensitive to my family's conflicts I probably, in a sense, infected myself. Later in my childhood, I began having lower back pain, too.

Despite my parents drug use, neglect, and inability to make me feel wanted, I knew that the land we lived on was magical. I felt cared for by an unknown source, and spent hours during childhood on the hillside by myself, in the long fading yellow grass. I'd say the "Our Father" prayer and ask God to stop my parents' fighting. I would lay on my back for what seemed like hours with my arms and legs spread open wide, watching the clouds pass by. I would look for angels, animals, and flowers in the shape of the clouds, and sometimes I would just fall asleep with the warmth of the Aussie hot sun on my face.

During my mum's Catholic upbringing, the nuns told her that to love yourself is a sin. Mum has strong spiritual inclinations, but with the darkness imparted by the church combined with being abused at home, I can only imagine what confusion arose in her young mind. While I was attending Catholic school, I could feel my mum getting madder and madder at her parents for sending me there. Finally, before I finished grade one, she put her foot down and enrolled me in public school.

During those years when my dad was in and out of jail for drug possession, my mum and I continued to move frequently. My dad says that the worst years of his life were during this time from 1985 to 1987, right around when my brother was born and I was about ten. My dad was busted three times and with the new "three strikes and you're out" law, he served three months of a six month jail sentence. While at home I never felt I was able to bring the few friends I made to our house for fear of being embarrassed by Mum's rage or her walking around naked or being high. When she was self-medicating with pot, though, she was more pleasant to be around. She was playful, nonjudgmental, and even enjoyed having me there, probably because she could be herself without feeling the pain. When she ran out of pot, the nightmare resumed. Because my dad wasn't around much, I would often fantasize about him picking me up and taking me to Dreamworld or Sea World like the other kids got to do.

Fishing for Worthiness

When I was seven, we moved to a Queensland suburb called Noosaville, and I entered grade three. I remember telling my teacher I had already attended eight primary schools and that my mother was a Rosicrucian. She looked at me strangely and asked, "What's that?" I told her I didn't know. I loved Noosaville. We rented an old, two-story home on the Noosa River, where everything is pristine and green. I wondered how long we'd be able to stay there, as I saw Mum getting antsy, not liking the small-town vibe.

I made friends with Beverly Clark, who lived around the corner. Her mum yelled a lot too, but it seemed more like sport than abuse. Beverly's father was a fisherman, and he would take his crew to Fraser, a beautiful white-sand island, when the fish were biting. I have great memories of days by the river with Beverly and her family. I learned about fish, bait, and tackle, and loved everything about it, even gutting, scaling, and cleaning the fish. Every chance I had, I was throwing out my hand-reel fishing line while taking in the earthy scent of the nearby eucalyptus trees. I'd fish in the early-morning hours, using prawns from the riverbed as bait. It was a great escape. I brought home fish to eat, usually whiting, flathead, and brim. Although I didn't have the support I needed from my parents, Mother Earth and Father Sky were always there looking after me.

Around this time, at eight years old, I had a horrific bicycle accident. And at the time it was awful, yet as I look back on it with an adult lens, it is a classic example of something happening *for* me and not *to* me, because without it, I may have not been on the journey toward deep healing as a practice that I'm on today. I was chasing Beverly down the Noosaville esplanade and my foot slipped off the petal and in a blink of an eye landed inside the spoke of the front wheel. Everything happening so fast—the bike and I flipped over like a circus trick and I landed on my back in the worst pain I'd ever had. I was crying out of control when the car that was behind me stopped and the driver carried me home. I probably went into some kind of shock because I don't remember feeling the pain again for months.

My dad visited us a couple of times in Noosaville. By then I'd built up a real hatred of him—and myself. One time I watched Dad turn the house upside down looking for a brick of gold from one of his drug deals. Mum had held it for him, then she wouldn't tell him where it was. He beat her up badly and threw furniture, plants, and clothes everywhere. I was stunned and shocked and didn't feel safe, afraid that they were going to yell at me next.

My sense of unworthiness got locked in at this stage. Maybe I took on my mum's pain. Needing to soothe myself, I grabbed a few coins, went to the corner store, and ate three ice creams along the river. As a preteen, I started putting on weight. I felt deprived and anxious, and carried these feelings into adulthood. I felt as though there's plenty of good stuff out there, but never enough for me—and I wasn't deserving anyway. I became resentful of the girls with mummies and daddies who cared for them. My body started hoarding weight beginning around this time of about nine years old, as I was trying, and failing, to control what was outside my control. I continued my disordered eating through my mid-twenties, the time I lived in Hollywood, where during certain periods I hardly ate at all.

All those years, I never spoke to anyone about how I was feeling, and never told my teachers what was going on at home. My schoolwork suffered. I was in remedial English, probably due to undiagnosed dyslexia, which certainly didn't help my lack of self-esteem and worthiness. I think my mum was just trying to hold things together so my schoolwork wasn't high on her list of concerns. During this time I would mostly get C's, and some B's.

Song and Dance

One time when I was around the age of nine, Papa and Mammiee visited us at the riverfront home. My grandpa was sickened by what he saw, and he called the police about my dad's drug dealing. Dad was busted shortly after that, arrested and sent to jail. When we visited him there, he told us jail was actually good for him, that he had lots of friends (he always made friends) and was learning to take care of himself through working out.

While Dad was in jail, it was pretty quiet at home. Mum met a man named Don Allen, who was old enough to be her father. He was a gentle soul, always nice to me. We'd sing together in the car, songs like "Mr. Sandman," "Fever," and "New York, New York," and he was supportive of my performing aspirations, calling me the Blond Bombshell. However, all that did was strengthen my false ego, and it didn't address my real sense of unworthiness. Still, I loved having a male role model and getting all that attention. He was a Burgher, a mixed-race descendant of Europeans who settled in Sri Lanka and married Sri Lankan women. But Mum seemed almost more unsettled if that is possible when he would come around. He always seemed suspicious of her seeing other people. I felt like I was in the middle of yet another relationship that wasn't working out.

It was Don who introduced my mum to the Rosicrucian Order, a spiritual movement based on esoteric Western traditions. My mum was a natural meditator. She was able to do it lying down in bed, and for years I would hear her say, "I'm going to meditate." When I was young, she read the children's versions of Rosicrucian books to me, but I just wasn't interested in them, or her.

The problem with Don was that he was married, though he and his wife Ellen may have had an understanding that allowed him to take a mistress. Ellen would prepare elaborate meals for us to take on picnics. Don was a highly regarded palm reader, and taught my mum everything about palmistry. Mum felt he was her soulmate. I wasn't allowed to talk to my grandparents about them. Papa didn't approve of Don, maybe because he was married, perhaps because he was twice my mum's age, or both. Once again, I was caught in the middle.

Before my brother Jason was born, I began dance classes when I was about eight years old. I loved singing and dancing! It was around this time that I won a place in a talent school operated by a TV station in Brisbane. But Mum was pregnant and driving almost two hours each way was out of the question, so instead I entered a local singing competition with kids throughout South East Queensland and came in second which was unbelievable to me. People clapped and smiled and looked as though they were enjoying themselves, and I loved every minute of it. For that moment, all my doubts and insecurities vanished. I still remember the song and its words. I sang "She Shall Have Music" (wherever she goes) and when I hear it today it reminds me of my grandmother and our bond through the love of music. We would often sing this song together just for fun after the competition.

Noosa Shire

When I was nine, Dad went to prison again, and he and my mum separated for good. Mum and I lived on Australia's government pension for single parents. It wasn't much that we lived on but she made it work. We moved to a farmhouse called Juanita, outside Cooroy, also in Noosa Shire. There was no electricity or plumbing, just an outhouse and a generator.

The only door was in the front of the house. As you entered, to the right was a shower and to the left the floorboards would creek as you walked to the kitchen. The outhouse was about twenty yards from the main house. It was scary to go out in the middle of the night to pee. My bedroom didn't have a door, and it was at this time of my life that I began to have pubic hair. I remember looking down at my private parts to investigate my changing body, opening my legs really wide and stretching my neck downward to examine myself, when Freddy, my mum's next boyfriend, walked around the corner and saw me. He was shocked, and I was horrified! That week he made a door for me. I was really grateful and realized how embarrassed I was. We never spoke about it. He just put the door on quietly and quickly. It was kind of him to realize my needs and jump on it so quickly.

I missed the river house, but adapted, as always, to the beautiful environs. This was to be my baby brother's first home, and Freddy drove us to the hospital where Jason was born. Freddy didn't stay, but I did. Mum was in labor all day, and I played around and pressed the drip button for her when it beeped. Mum asked for me to be at her bedside for the birth, but the nurses disagreed, and thank goodness. My grandparents drove down from Brisbane and arrived to view Mum in a wheelchair just out of the delivery room. I was really happy to see them. It was a lot for a nine-year-old.

Freddy lived with us for a short time in Juanita. He was a lovely, gentle guy, and it was quiet when he was there. I remember Mum saying, after he was gone, that he needed to find someone to have his own kids with.

About a year after Jason was born, when I was ten, we moved from Juanita into a smaller home on Ada Street in Tewantin, still in Noosa Shire. I think I must have been exhausted from the moving, but at least everything worked well; the house wasn't falling apart like Juanita, although there were lots of mosquitoes in the area, and we all had mosquito nets over our beds. This house was closer to the shops, and I could ride my bike to school. It was also walking distance from an odd attraction called the House of Bottles, which was built completely from bottles and housed a collection of unusual and historic bottles. I would escape there and look around, even though it was tiny and I never saw anything new.

My grandparents liked the Ada Street house and visited often. When my grandparents were there or on their way, Mum would leave the laundry basket on our car, outside and in the open, to let Don Allen know not to come in—he was still in the picture. One time I walked in on Don in the bathroom as he was washing his penis. I didn't have a clue what he was doing and just ran away. He smiled and said, "Hello, Mellara," and that was it. It was in this house he and Mum began arguing. I think she was feeling suffocated by his asking where she'd been or where she was going or why she didn't pick up the phone. I never could understand their love-hate relationship.

We lived there for about a year and then moved to a farmhouse on ten acres near Lake Cooroibah. On weekends, Mum would palm-read at the Eumundi Markets, and I'd stay home with Jason. I *loved* being a big sister, having someone to take care of. When I wasn't playing too hard, practically killing him with affection, I continued to yearn for stability and belonging.

Mum let me go off to be with my dad for two weeks, the only time I remember living with him while I was growing up. He seemed to be well financially; I felt proud of him. Maybe Mum finally received some money from him and I was allowed to go, because I don't know why she would have let me do this. She was always complaining that he never gave any "maintenance," the Australian equivalent of child support, toward my upbringing. He had a beautiful apartment, and his girlfriend took me shopping. She also turned on a porn video that was in the recorder and started playing it. I don't think she had been around kids before because she left it on and I didn't know what I was watching but just went back to my coloring anyway. I remember a drug raid during this visit. Dad jumped out of bed naked with his hands up, surrounded by police. They opened up the attic and pot started falling from the ceiling. It was awful seeing him like that.

With Mum's support, I enrolled in a modeling and commercial agency, landed a few jobs—Dreamworld, Seven National News—and posed for some modeling brochures. The acting bug was growing in me, or maybe it was that the little Mellara inside of me was receiving praise and what I thought of as love, and I would do anything to get more of that.

I got my first period when I was thirteen. I was out shopping with a girlfriend, bought a pad, and proceeded to use it. Mum had never shown me how; I had to figure it out for myself. Eventually I told her, and she was happy, saying, "You're a woman now!" I didn't understand what she meant. A few days later she bought me some pads, and I still didn't know what to do. So I used them all and she got angry and started belittling me. "Why'd you use them all? What've you been doing, eating them?" She laughed her head off and walked away. I felt so unsupported, unloved, and profoundly sad. As a sensitive child, I was often broken by her words and deeds. When I look at my mum now, I can only imagine the many ways her mother may have not helped her either.

First #MeToo Moment

After the school year of 1989, while I was staying with my grandparents in Brisbane, I enrolled in a summer acting program. One day while I was waiting for Mum to pick me up—I was the last student there, by myself—I was standing and talking to the instructor, a middle-aged, long-faced, skinny-legged creep wearing a Hawaiian shirt that seemed two sizes too small with his belly hanging out. Then suddenly, he reached for my breast and grabbed it as though he was turning a doorknob. He did it with such entitlement and a look on his face like this was something normal. It wasn't an accident, quickly bounced off with apologies. He was practically touching my rib cage. I pushed his hand away. I felt so violated and disgusted, and I was in shock. He said, "Haven't you seen me looking at you?" like it was somehow my fault for not knowing his mind. I went home and didn't tell anybody, but didn't go back to the summer acting program again. To this day, I still feel his physical and energetic violation.

To make matters worse, my mother said, "I don't think you're gifted enough to be an actress. You just weren't born that way. Actors are born, and you're not one of them." I cried for days. All I wanted was to be seen and supported. At one screaming match with lots of crying I told her, "I want nothing of you!" and she yelled back, "You'll need your mother one day." That's strange, I thought, because I needed her now. I was determined to leave home as soon as I could.

When Mum had enough of living in Noosa, my grandparents helped her apply for government assistance to build a home under a new program for single parents. Parcels of land on Tamborine Mountain with a full view of the Gold Coast were reasonably priced in 1987, and soon this was our reality. Mum, Papa, Mammiee, and I worked hard, painting the inside and doing everything we could to make it beautiful and comfy. With housing and Mum's stay-at-home pension, our basic physical needs were met.

But we were still living below the poverty level, and I desperately wanted to change my life's trajectory. So I applied for a job at the Eagle Heights Café, a local bakery and ice cream shop. I told the café owner I was sixteen and she hired me. I loved earning money and the freedom it brought. I was able to buy some things I wanted like trendy clothes, shoes, and some make-up just

like all the other girls my age. I also did modeling and commercials. Eighteen years later, when I was pregnant with my husband
Mike's and my first child, I went back to the Eagle Heights Café
with him, and the same owner was there. She told Mike not to
believe anything I said—that she knew I'd lied about my age—
and then she added I was the hardest, most enjoyable worker
she'd ever had.

CHAPTER TWO

La La Land

At the tender age of fifteen, looking older than my years and slathering myself with makeup, I got involved with a TV and film producer twenty years my senior—practically my dad's age! He took me on shopping trips in Sydney, and we stayed in his apartment overlooking the Sydney Opera House and Harbour Bridge. At other times, we stayed at his penthouse on the Gold Coast, with a 360-degree view from the bay to the hinterland. He'd pick me up from school in his BMW convertible, and told me our relationship was a fairytale, like Charles and Diana's, and that I was lucky to be with him. I thought he was right. I immersed myself in materialism and a feeling of being loved that—for a period of time—masked my childhood angst. I had always tried to find myself in other people's expectations, and this was a fit. I was living a dream I thought was my own.

Through their inaction, my beloved grandparents allowed me to be with him, mesmerized by his wealth and power, I suppose. And my mum didn't intervene either. Maybe it was because I was so headstrong. I would battle her over every ounce of control she tried to exert. I was disrespectful and blamed her for my pain, just as my parents had blamed each other.

Only when I began writing this book did I realize this relationship with an older man was not consensual. I was attracted to him and initiated the contact, so I always felt it had been my responsibility, a youthful fantasy and a sexual fling. But when # MeToo stories became a worldwide conversation in the fall of 2017, I realized that the power and age differences made our being together inappropriate. It took #MeToo becoming a worldwide phenomenon before I saw that I was part of a collective energy, and began my healing process.

I first laid eyes on him during a plane trip from Queensland to Sydney. He looked handsome and powerful. I'd never been on a plane before and was excited just to be flying. He was sitting next to a well-known actress, and I rushed over and introduced myself to both of them. I was a fan of hers and a budding actress myself. He gave me his card and said I should look him up the next time I was in Sydney.

It was Australian summer, the end of November 1990. I had just finished tenth grade. My family and I were en route to Western Australia, where we'd spend six weeks, including Christmas, so my six-year-old brother could meet his birth father. We'd always thought my dad was Jason's father, but as he began to grow up, Mum could see otherwise, and DNA tests proved it. I didn't want to wait till the end of summer to be in touch with this man, so as soon as we landed in Sydney to change planes, I phoned him, and he invited us to his TV pre/post-production offices. Because we had a four-hour layover, Mum, Jason, and I were able to jump into a cab and go right over. I saw maybe thirty people working on a good handful of shows, and I was hooked. I wanted to be a part of it!

At the end of the summer, when we returned from Western Australia, he contacted me and the romance began with lavish dinners, shopping trips, gala affairs, you name it. I wasn't exactly in love with him, but I was starving for attention and wanted to be with him—always. At fifteen I started staying over at his homes, and at sixteen, I left Mum and moved in with him. I thought he was my ticket out of suffering. When I was with him, I felt less lonely, but every time I got clingy, his reactions were strange. He became moody and verbally abusive. There were times I lay on his marble-tiled bathroom floor for hours, crying. After walking on eggshells my whole childhood, all I wanted was peace, and ironically my choices gave me the opposite. I was with him on and off for the next two and a half years.

Tinseltown

When childhood becomes unbearable, we develop fantasies to avoid feeling the pain. Because I loved the arts—singing, acting, and dancing—and craved attention from audiences, I envisioned myself an international actress hanging out with Nicole Kidman and other Australian stars, and winning an Oscar. So, after graduating high school, I went for broke! It was my moment. With stars in my eyes, I applied to the Lee Strasberg Theatre Institute in Los Angeles, and was accepted. I'd also been accepted to attend Queensland University, but I chose Hollywood. I felt if I could make it there, I could make it anywhere, so why stay in my boring backyard? I was seventeen, and it was goodbye and good luck to everything I knew in beautiful Australia.

Because I was not yet eighteen, I had to get my dad to sign a consent. I found him in an apartment on the Gold Coast on a couch with another guy rolling a joint, laughing and getting high, so I didn't say too much. He signed the papers and said to me, "Don't be a stranger." For five years I'd been going to a high school a stone's throw from where he lived, and he never tried to see me. But, now, as I was about to leave for the other side of the world, he said don't be a stranger. How strange, I thought.

Splash

"If you want to get run over by a freight train, you have to be on the tracks!" a Hollywood photographer said to me during my first photo shoot. I was not yet eighteen. After the shoot, he took me to the home of the highly acclaimed film producer Robert Evans of *The Godfather* fame.

The photographer had me stand beside the pool while he went inside to get the producer. I was wearing tight blue jeans and a white T-shirt. With a strong Aussie accent, I said, "Nice to meet you, Mr. Evans." He looked at the photographer and said, "Nice. Reminds me of Michelle Pfeiffer." It felt like they were in a butcher shop looking over a piece of Aussie meat. At the same time, I loved the attention!

We went back into the photographer's car, and he told me he needed some pictures of me naked before he could recommend me for acting parts, and reluctantly I agreed. This was typical for me, saying yes, then chickening out at the last minute. A few days later I took my shirt off for the photo shoot, and then he told me to wet my hair in the kitchen sink to make it look like a shower scene. I did, and then he said that it was time to take everything off. I felt nervous and said I wasn't ready, and he started to yell at me. So I collected my things and my composure and never saw him again. Later, I did undress for some parts in movies because at the time it felt like the only way to get a break.

Balance

We all have something to remind us to live in balance. For me it's back pain. A few months after the horrendous bicycle accident when I was eight, I injured myself again trying a high kick in dance class. I didn't feel much pain in my back after that, until I was twenty and living in LA. Fortunately, Mum and Jason, who was eleven at the time, were visiting. After a series of rigorous classes at the Strasberg School, I was unable to walk, the pain was so excruciating. I got an MRI, and the doctors said all five lower discs in my back were protruding three to four millimeters and hitting nerve endings, enough protrusion to create unbearable pain but not enough for surgery. One doctor said he'd never seen that much degeneration in someone my age.

Although the pain seemed to show up out of the blue, I know now it was many years in the making. In addition to the bike accident and dance class kick, feeling unsupported was a huge contributing factor. I'd never learned to cherish myself or receive the love I so dearly needed. So my body spoke to me with this disease to shine light on how defeated I felt and to encourage me to turn my life around.

Right before Jason was born, when I was nine, Mum took a correspondence course and became a naturopathic physician. She would always try new things on me like homeopathic remedies, supplements, and flower essences. She was really generous in that regard, and just being around her I became knowledgeable in these areas. But when I really needed to see a Western doctor for something, I experienced her as, to say the least, not supportive.

Although I was holding on to my dream of becoming an actress, my life had become untenable. It felt as though my spirit had been taken away, and I sank into a deep depression. I'd never been on meds, and taking muscle relaxants and strong pain relievers was the last thing I wanted to do, but I had to escape the pain. Ultimately, debilitating back pain led me to a life-healing path. Without it, I never would have found my life's purpose. But in the short run, it almost triggered an addiction to painkillers.

For a few days, I was unable to walk, and Mum and Jason helped me get around. My older boyfriend paid the bills, but it was increasingly stressful to be around him. I knew I would have to support myself if I was going to get away from him. Once my mum and brother left the country to go back to their lives in Australia, I used my days to look for a waitressing job. I must have applied to about ten restaurants in the same area on Melrose Avenue, in Hollywood. I got hired almost instantly to be a hostess at one of them, and they said when a waiting job became available, they would consider me.

From the beginning of that job I started to put money aside so that I could leave him and pay for my own apartment. When I had enough money for the first month's rent, I packed up my things with the help of my best girlfriend that I met at Strasberg and moved into a place with three other roommates just walking distance to the restaurant. Only later did I discover that he was bilking investors to come up with the money for his lavish life-style. Later that year, when I was well enough to visit Australia, five or six plainclothes Australian Federal Police met me at the Sydney Airport. I was startled, but thankful to discover they weren't after me. They recognized I was another casualty of this man's choices. They asked a few questions, and I was able to catch my plane to Brisbane, where Mum and my grandparents met me. Mum, always excited to see me, greeted me warmly. But after the excitement wore off, she became condescending and snarky, as always.

First Marriage

When I got back to LA, I was confronted by how hard it was to be in a place where everything's different from home, except for the common language, and I thought about giving up on Hollywood and returning to Australia to attend Queensland University. It's a well-respected school, and earning a degree would have made my family proud, especially my grandparents. If I had, I probably would have gotten bored and returned back to the States. The US represented freedom for me. I felt I could do anything there and become whatever I put my mind to. I didn't always feel that in Australia. There, it feels like everyone's kind of in their place and can't move too far outside that, or at least that was my young person's prospective at the time. On the flip side of that coin, there is also a deep mateship and community-feeling that the rest of the world knows us for and that distinctly makes us Aussies, well, *Aussies*. A "mate" is more than just a friend and it implies a sense of shared responsibility, experience, and mutual respect. But probably because I didn't develop a secure attachment with my parents, I may have seemed to be a rebel when it came to mateship back then. Not that my love for Australia or Australians was gone from my heart, but I felt separate, unloved and unwanted. If I had gone back to Australia it would have been more of the suffocation I felt growing up and just wanting to get out and be somewhere completely different and far away.

At the time, I was dating Tommy, the manager of the restaurant on Melrose Avenue where I worked. We were only dating just a few weeks and I knew I had found my next boyfriend. He was so passionate about me, perhaps a little on the intense side, but I liked it all the same. And he was much closer to my age, only seven years older than me. I also loved that he was the man in charge of the restaurant, which made him even more sexy than he already was. During a long night of waiting tables, he was always giving me loving glances from across the room. I felt so seen by him, especially when we would have beautiful people come in from the local Hollywood studios and he would only have his eyes on me, and no one else. He also had that tall, dark, and handsome look in spades, so far from the iconic blonde-haired beachy look that I was used to growing up. So when he saw that I was seriously considering returning to Australia, he proposed, saying, "Please stay. I love you," and "We'll make it work." I was eighteen and I said yes. Tommy's mom, stepdad, and half-sister thought I must be pregnant for us to be getting married so quickly. I found a dress I just loved at the Beverly Center, LA's fashion Mecca, that cost $500. I'd never spent that much on a dress with my own money. Tommy invited all his friends, and we had a ceremony with about fifty guests at his mother's home in a wealthy LA suburb.

None of my family was present. Tommy and his mom's relationship was strained, but I found her to be sweet, and I really liked this family. And they seemed happy to see me with him. A year after our wedding, his mom and her husband paid my way back to visit Australia.

Love Boat: The Next Wave

At nineteen, I got my Screen Actors Guild (SAG) card, which meant I was somebody agents could consider a serious actress. After that I was in two B movies, but mostly got rejection after rejection. I did star in one movie, and played a small part as Peter Fonda's girlfriend in another, the 1996 movie *Don't Look Back*. But after these jobs I began to lose interest as I wasn't booking anything. I couldn't discern any reason for this other than Hollywood has never been known for any kind of job security, although I will admit I was totally run by my emotions and could be impulsive. But that feeling or phase didn't last long, kind of like anything in my life. So I decided to give acting another try. I quit my job at the restaurant and auditioned for a stand-in role for a new *Love Boat* TV series, and I got it! It was a huge opportunity; I was finally going to be around the film industry on a daily basis. And as a SAG union member, I had the security of healthcare for Tommy and me.

With the *Love Boat* crew, I travelled to the Caribbean, Mexico, and Jamaica. I loved being on location, but things at home were rough. Tommy acted manic, sometimes loving and caring and other times just plain mean and all over the shop. As a result, I became the breadwinner as he was increasingly unable to handle stress. He'd belittle me, yell at me, and even spit on my face, energy I knew too well. I fought back, which only made things worse.

In addition to the *Love Boat* job, I went back to working at the restaurant when the show was on hiatus. Tommy and I also managed two apartment buildings in exchange for rent. The first was low-income housing, filled mostly with unstable people, many on government assistance. The tenants knocked on our door all hours of the day and night for problems ranging from being locked out to leaky faucets to bug infestations. I was at my lowest ebb, and Tommy could barely function.

Waitressing on my feet for hours, my lower back pain was out of control. I would lay on the restaurant's bathroom floor next to the toilet in a sea of tears, crying for things to change, just as I did on my first boyfriend's marble floor a few years before. I'd call my mum in the middle of her night searching for answers, but she didn't know how to soothe me either. That just brought up more things to be sad about. My grandpa would tell me, "Just come home, Love," and if I couldn't afford the airfare, Qantas

Airways gave tickets to Australian citizens who needed to get home.

One afternoon, I was taking a hot bath, my back was killing me, and I felt especially low, like I was nothing—I had come from nothing and had come to nothing. Life—something outside myself—was beating me up, and I was mad at God, my family, and myself for how my life had turned out. If I were succeeding as an actress, I thought, everything would be all right. But instead, my life was a mess.

I needed to take some Soma and Vicodin to quell the pain, and in the bath, agitated and unsettled, I swallowed a handful of pills, cupping my hands and using the spout from the tub to get them down with some water. When you mix these two painkillers, I've since learned, it's called a Las Vegas Cocktail and has an effect like heroin. As I was swallowing them, I began thinking I'd be better off dead as my life was just too painful. So I kept cupping my hands for water and taking more pills; I lost count of how many. Then I got scared and realized I'd done something horrible.

I thought that taking sleeping pills would help me calm down and make everything better, so I got out of the tub, looked in the medicine cabinet, and took six or eight Tylenol PMs. I started to feel dizzy and my vision got blurry. I got even more scared and wished I hadn't done what I'd just done. Tommy was in the other room and I came out naked and disoriented, by then unable to see at all even though my eyes were open. The next thing I remember was being placed into the back of an ambulance and (my sight must have returned) looking up at the window of our apartment. Just as I'd seen our other crazy tenants being carried off, now I was one of them.

I must have passed out again, as I remember waking up in an LA hospital with my stomach being pumped. I was looking down to the side of the bed I was on and seeing black stuff coming out of the tube. It was disgusting, and the pain was worse than my back pain had ever been. The doctor was trying to get it down lower inside of me, and I realized in that moment—like a movie of my life was playing out—how silly I was to do this to myself.

I was so hard on myself, and just wanted to have this mess I'd created go away.

I was in ICU for twenty-four hours, hearing the haunting howls of an elderly woman next to me. She was expressing exactly how I felt—cut off from the world. Tommy visited a few times, but mostly I was there by myself and so was able to look at what I'd done. The hospital psychiatrist wasn't convinced I was okay to leave, and rightfully so. I remember trying to convince him I was AOK and that I'd never do this to myself again. I was relocated to what I thought was the psychiatric care section of the hospital and stayed for four long days until they felt I was psychologically sound and not a threat to myself. I never told my family that I tried to kill myself. I felt ashamed at what I had done—it was quite unbelievable to me that I took things that far.

I was depressed and feeling quite alone after this and spent almost every day for a few years healing for an hour at the Korean baths just around the corner from us. I had heard from a friend that they would be good for my back, and they were. For fifteen dollars for admission I would go from the hot to the cold bath, from the dry sauna to the steam sauna, kind of like a meditation. The Korean women taught me how to scrub my body and like a family they would sometimes scrub my back for me. That's what we did for each other, even if we didn't know the person that well. I began to learn a few words in their language, but I wasn't very good at it. They were welcoming to me and it was good for me to be by myself to process my feelings in a safe environment. I had found a place of refuge in the city where I felt I belonged. There weren't many folks who looked like me going there, mostly Korean women, given its location in Korea Town. These beautiful women would offer me fruit and whatever they were eating at the baths which made me feel so happy and included.

I never brought anyone to my special bathing place in the city, mostly because I was still healing and I needed a place where I could be quiet. What I learned most about this time in my life is that I needed to start taking much better care of myself physically, mentally, and emotionally. As I became stronger and mentally healthier, I made a vow to myself that I would never do something so harmful like swallowing pills again. I also begin therapy from someone who was already helping a friend who I knew. She was an intern in training to be a therapist which meant that I only had her for a few months but I paid her very little compared to a fully licensed therapist. It was extremely helpful and it worked well for me. She helped me to understand that what I was going through was normal especially given my upbringing. I didn't know this at the time but this was my slow introduction to accepting myself as I am.

Beautifully Crafted Positions

Around this time, another friend introduced me to yoga to see if it would be a support to my back. She took me to Quantum Yoga which had just opened (it later became City Yoga and is now YogaWorks West Hollywood), and we were the only students in class. The teacher was good, but it was excruciating for me to get into the postures. Yoga seemed slow, and I knew it wasn't for me. I wanted a quick fix for my emotional and physical pain.

After the insurance money that covered my physical therapy ran its course, I gave yoga another try. I was in deep trouble on all levels and needed a way to mend. This time when I assumed the first posture, I felt a profound release in my body, like a newborn being sweetly caressed by her mum, and there was no turning back. Stopping to feel the quiet within and watching myself open up, I fell in love with the newfound ease and visited *every* yoga studio in LA, taking classes with so many great teachers.

It was a gift to move in these beautifully crafted positions and quiet the chatter of my mind. Areas that had been blocked, tight, or injured began to open. Exhales felt like bridges connecting my body, mind, and heart with my breath. It was like entering the heartbeat of the Mother. In the deep quiet, I could feel her soothing me. I embraced a oneness within myself and with all beings I can only describe it as *pure love*, the biggest hug from the most beautiful being in the cosmos. I've continued practicing ever since. With yoga, I have the patience and resources to tackle whatever comes up, including the recurrent pain in my back. Today I would tell that young woman in pain, "You'll manage. You'll move through this, and it won't be as consuming as it feels today."

My favorite studio was the Center for Yoga on Larchmont (now YogaWorks Larchmont). It was the first yoga studio to open in LA. I went to class there every day and usually the Korean sauna after that. The yoga studio had such a good feeling; it was beautifully maintained by the manager, Gary, and his partner, Christine. They took great care of me and considered me part of their family, offering me a job there so I could take classes and not pay. I worked the front desk, mopped floors, and signed people into class. I loved the discipline of folding the blankets a certain way and taking care of the space. It was extremely healing for me. I had found home.

When the *Love Boat* came back from hiatus, I was back to my stand-in gig where essentially my job was to be lit by the lighting crew and Director of Photography so that the actors can have the time to become "camera ready." I liked my job and the money was really good. As we started in the new season I began to receive attention from one of the show's stars. He was going through a lot in his life and was very supportive of me, genuinely asking how I was doing and about yoga. If he was flirting, I didn't realize it, and he made no advances. There was a rumor that I was with him, but it was far from the truth.

I was, however, intrigued by one of the directors on board. I enjoyed his energy, and we talked a lot. It's easy to become close on set, because we're all like one happy family. On location, he and I were staying on the same deck of the ship, and he told me he'd leave his door cracked open for me. Once inside his room, he gave me a cocktail and we sat for a little bit and he told me how he wasn't connecting with his wife much anymore. He said he was looking for a girlfriend, someone he could be with outside his marriage. We started to kiss, and he very quickly pulled down his pants and exposed himself. I should have seen where this was heading, but it was all too quick for me. I wasn't stupid, just really startled, and I ran back to my room.

The next day it was awkward on set, but he was still flirting as if nothing had happened. This was the end of our filming on location. The rest of the project was on sound stages. I was happy to get off the boat and be in Hollywood with a different director. During postproduction, that director reached out to me again, and I was tempted. He told me he could see me doing a few parts in the next series he was working on, and asked me out for lunch. I didn't go; I just wasn't ready to bring in that kind of drama by having a relationship with a married man in hopes that it would bring me acting work. It seemed to happen all the time with folks on set, but it just wasn't my thing.

Tommy and I moved into the other apartment building we co-managed, and I threw myself into acting. I still had the *Love Boat* gig and got two on-camera acting roles as well. I was due on set at 6 a.m. and sometimes wouldn't return home till 9 or 10 p.m. I was building relationships outside of my union with Tommy. I knew that if I was going to have the strength to leave him, I would need another boyfriend to jump to. That was my pattern—security and love at all costs. During the long shooting days, I would bring my yoga mat and find a corner on stage where it was dark and I wouldn't be noticed practicing yoga. On the weekends and during the series' hiatus, I immersed myself in yoga classes all around the Los Angeles area. Back then there were no iPhones to help with directions, just the old school Thomas Guide for directions. And for a yoga fanatic like me, there were a handful of cardboard yoga flyers from every studio in the area. I would drive everywhere for yoga and I began apprenticing with yoga teacher Steven Freedman once a week.

One Friday I decided that this was the time to leave Tommy and was packed up and out by Monday without saying a word to him. I just left. It was months in the making—his inability to take better care of himself emotionally, his attacks on me personally, and his changeable moods just had become too much. It was maybe six months later that I met him at a gas station parking lot to apologize, and it would be the last time we saw each other. He seemed very dressed up with a crisp button-up shirt and jeans. I also noticed that he had capped all of his front teeth and his hair looked beautiful, all wavy and attractive. I think he was trying to show me that he had changed and was taking better care of himself. I think he would have liked it if we got back together, but it was a little too late for me. I had already moved on, and yet it was still very sad.

Ideas of Perfection

Back pain happens to many people, the result of an accident or something congenital or simply from sitting badly. For me, having a daily practice of yoga, compassion, and living in awareness is the best preventative medicine. As Oprah might say, these efforts help me live my best life now! Listening to my body's mind with sensitivity, I'm able to discern which postures are needed. Staying aware is a daily, sometimes hourly effort.

I had been harsh on my body, not listening to what it needed, pushing its limits, and as a result, creating pain. When the pain was triggered by an emotion, I'd be tough on myself, restricting my food intake and reinforcing messages that I'm not good enough, which only worsened it. I was a conspirator in my own self-destruction, unable to feel gratitude for all that my body gives me. I could only see what it wasn't able to do, and it hurt.

I am not as harsh on my body as I was back then, but I still have moments where I have to consciously find what is working so well in my body and focus on that. It has taken me years, even decades to get where I am today. With each day I am realizing that to love my body is to meet my body where it is. Now when my back injury flares up, I slow down, observe my breathing, and visualize sending healing waves of peace throughout my body. Some of my physical injuries I believe are connected to old thoughts that I have perceived as true and sometimes they can be triggered in the present moment. When this happens I try to be aware of it and if possible where the root of the triggering is coming from. And if I don't have an answer, I try not to push for it because healing usually comes on its own timeline and when we least expect it to. So when I am having an intense moment I remind myself that none of us have it all worked out. Some of us are just trying to get through the day and continue to work on self-love. I'll simply witness what's present in my body, like what sensations am I feeling. Or I will take a walk outside for a few minutes, a few times in a day, and close my eyes with the sun on my face, taking in its warmth. And if a breeze rolls on by I will give thanks to the universe that I stopped to remember the fullness of my inner beauty and my life. Having this tool of awareness in my back pocket has been a game changer for me and it helps me to return to the moment and love myself. We're most at-risk when we lose self-awareness.

Through yoga, meditation, and concentration, I'm now able to stay aware of my body and see what it needs. I'm not perfect, and some days it still flares up. But through mindful awareness, I can come up with a healing action plan to see me through, and hopefully I won't need surgery. I try to stay open to the flow of life and be present with what comes my way. Of course, I have ideas of what I'd like to happen, but I acknowledge that the *discrepancy* between my desire for what is and isn't actually going on is what brings suffering. Every day I find that I'm working to have a better relationship with the moment, and, when I remember to do this, there is a sense of ease or flow that feels magical.

I've learned that when the mind wants the body to perform like a circus animal, abusing it and trying to bring about someone's idea of perfection, it's a collision course. Sometimes the body needs rest; sometimes it gets sick, which can be a release of sorts. The mind can disturb the homeostasis of the body through its demands. In this sense, getting sick might be considered a gift. The opportunity in this moment is to slow down, and be the observer, looking for any negative thoughts we might have. When we have them, we mistreat the body, and we can recalibrate and return home to *what is* once our awareness catches the thought in midair, or mid-sentence, if you will. Like any practice, this is a practice to keep practicing. Just by shining our light of awareness onto these habitual thought patterns, a feeling of freedom of mind and caring of our body is within reach.

I studied Hatha, Viniyoga, Iyengar, and Ashtanga yoga, and at twenty-two, after studying with Steven Freedman, Steve Walther, Diana Beardsley, Marla Apt, Paul Cabanis, and Frank White, all highly skilled, I became a yoga teacher. A few years later, I continued my teacher training with Erich Shiffmann and Saul David Raye, and established a private and a studio practice in Westlake Village. Teaching yoga contributed greatly to my self-healing, and I've been able to light a spark in others for their healing too. I'm forever grateful for the pain I've had to endure, as it helps bring me to the truth of who I am and how actions have consequences. This injury and inquiry will be with me the rest of my life.

Second Marriage

I met Ben—who became my second husband—while I was working on *Love Boat*. We knew we'd be together when I was ready to move out on Tommy. Ben had bought his first house when he was nineteen with a loan from his father, and I loved that he was young, rich, and in a secure position working for his dad. His family was successful and influential in the film industry; his dad was the kindest man I knew.

Getting to know Ben was a happy time for me. He was three years younger than I and, in a way, reminded me of my little brother, a sweet boy with loads of energy and ready for fun. Ben loved being with me, too. He called me hot, and his friends couldn't believe he'd landed me. Pretty yes, but I could never see my worthiness beyond my good looks that I was given. I was trying hard to be more than me, to be accepted. I was already accepted, but I didn't know it or couldn't feel it.

Ben drove a big pick-up truck with huge wheels. Sometimes on weekends he'd ride his motorbike in the sand dunes at Pismo Beach. It was great fun to be with him. I should have left it at that and just had fun, but because I needed to hold on and be looked after, we ended up marrying.

After filming for *Love Boat* was over, I continued teaching yoga and trying out for acting parts. I came close to getting a recurring role on *Beverly Hills, 90210*. I made it all the way to producers, but in the end, I didn't get the part and was devastated. Ben had a job with a major TV show, and I felt envious. I wished I could be there with him. I was codependent, calling him and leaving him messages all day long.

When Ben asked me to move in with him, I said only if we were engaged to be married. I don't know where I got that from, but I meant business, and his mom loved it! One time while Ben and I were on a hike on the trails around Malibu, he presented me with a family-heirloom engagement ring. He didn't get down on one knee, but I loved that it was under the open sky.

Moving in with him was a kind of consolation prize after being rejected from *Beverly Hills, 90210*. I didn't want to be tethered to uncertainty any longer, and in that moment, I decided I'd had enough of acting. If I couldn't get the parts I auditioned for, I was happy to marry into one. I was confused and loved the idea of a family and husband to save me. Truthfully, he wasn't ready to be married and neither was I. But his family took me in as though I was always meant to be their daughter-in-law.

His mother especially loved the idea. She also seemed controlling at times because later when we were on our honeymoon in Hawaii, she came into our house and organized my closet and underwear drawer. She probably thought she was being helpful, but it felt strange to me, and I didn't have the confidence to say anything. To be fair, she had three boys whom she did everything for and perhaps she was including me in with them. But I was never used to someone doing that kind of thing for me, let alone a mother. During the holidays, I loved the gifts his parents gave me. Most of all, I loved the attention. His mom had always wanted a daughter, and she lavished me with what I thought was love. She had a doll collection, and now I think I was just another one of them to her.

A turning point in my relationship with Ben was when he told me he'd had an affair with the star of the show where he worked. I was uncontrollably jealous and sick to my stomach. That's when

I became determined to marry him! Such a stupid reason to marry someone. Of course, I had other reasons to marry him, but I didn't like that he went off somewhere else. I wanted to be the *only* star in his eyes. We ended up marrying at a gorgeous, historic estate on a bluff overlooking the Pacific Ocean, practically a royal wedding.

Honeymoon's Over

Ben sold his house, and we bought a home together. My credit was bad from a bankruptcy with Tommy a few years earlier. Tommy was $35,000 in debt and convinced me that it was best for us to file for bankruptcy together. Now buying a home with Ben, I couldn't be listed on the loan as our mortgage rates would have been too high. Ben's mother encouraged us to include my name on the deed, not the loan. He agreed, and we did it. I was earning a living as a yoga teacher and felt I deserved co-owner-ship of the house. Ben offered a huge gift, the security of his full-time job that allowed me to spread my wings and focus on yoga.

At twenty-three, my yoga teaching was taking off. I was in love with all my students, happy to help each of them, and so in love with yoga, as it was healing my lower back and my soul, and offering me a place in the world. I became a well-established yoga teacher in the Westlake Village area, and I also had private students all over Malibu, the Valley, and Westlake. I was given the opportunity to teach a well-known musician at her home and on her US tour. She and I worked closely togetherfor almost a year. We were inseparable. On the road, we were bunkbed buddies. She had just gone through a breakup, and yoga was her medicine along with searching for a new spiritual bookstore every day as we toured the US.

The honeymoon phase of my marriage with Ben wound down in just a few months, when I started to see his dark side. He would punch the wall of our bedroom when he didn't agree with something I said. For me, that was normal and didn't set off any alarms. I was actually at the time unconsciously pushing his buttons to see how far things might go. I was so filled with anger, I was looking for trouble—driving fast, tailgating, walking around with a huge chip on my shoulder. Practicing Hatha Yoga intensely gave me an outlet to discharge the pent-up rage, but the same patterns and choices were playing out in my life again. In this way, even yoga can be an addiction, when it's used not to explore and discover what's within, but to avoid feeling the pain, a kind of spiritual bypass.

The family I'd married into wasn't supportive of my life separate from Ben, and Ben felt threatened by my freedom and success. "We built you an expensive yoga room," his mother told me, "even with a wall of ropes. Why would you need to teach outside?" They prevented me from traveling to Europe with the musician, which essentially ended my connection with her. In response, I moved toward yoga and away from Ben and his family.

At this point, I was smoking pot practically every night. It was all I could do not to feel the deep emotions that were rising up. I got high, then woke up and started again. I needed to leave Ben—the writing was on the wall—but the deeper truth was that I needed to see the harm I was bringing both of us by not living in awareness. Instead, I found ways to fight with him. It was a vicious cycle, and I fell into a deep depression.

I was teaching a private yoga class to a dear friend, and she told me, "Ben is just mean." As soon as she said it, I began to cry. She was right, and I needed to act. I'm so grateful for her courage to speak the difficult truth. Ben and I were married for just ten months, and together less than three years. On our last night together, I was hitting him uncontrollably, saying, "I hate you, I hate you, I hate you!" projecting some of the rage at my dad and the world onto him. We had a huge fight and two of my ribs got dislocated. I took my passport and ran out. Later, when he wasn't home, I went back in and gathered my belongings. By then, even though I was still doing yoga, my body was so weak, like skin and bones. I had hit rock bottom and was in a terrible cycle, again the victim. I knew I needed to stop. With advice from a friend, I obtained a restraining order, and his family completely disowned me.

Gofer

When I left acting, in addition to pursuing yoga intensely, I continued a weekly job as office manager for acclaimed director and photographer Elyse Lewin. Mostly she was hired for family and baby commercials and still photography. I was really her gofer; I helped her office run smoothly and did whatever else was needed. She saw that I was kind, a rare quality in Hollywood, and that I worked really hard, and she paid me well. She was like a mother to me. I saw myself in her too—always truthful, letting me know how she saw things, not sugar-coating anything. I treated her like a queen, making sure she had whatever she needed. Working with Elyse helped me gain confidence. She helped me in so many ways during the break-up with Ben. She was an anchor in the storm, a counselor offering pearls of heartfelt wisdom and practical advice.

Elyse was also a taskmaster. When I'd mess up, she'd get mad at me. I hated not doing things perfectly for her, yet appreciated the constructive criticism. She even took me to Russia for a job she had directing a Pampers ad. She told me I was really good with babies—I was able to get them laughing—and she knew she could count on me. I knew she cared about me and could see how broken I was. She taught me how to run her office, pay the bills, and a thousand other things. And I learned a lot just by watching her.

Choices

My life after leaving Ben was awful. I remember calling his grandmother, whom I felt close to, and telling her I was sorry for my part of what happened. She told me, firmly, "I'm sorry it went this far, Mellara. It's too bad," and she hung up. That day driving on the Simi Valley Freeway, I saw what my life had come to and felt completely alone. I was on my way to teach at Westlake Yoga, and had nothing to give.

Elyse gave me all the support she could. And I'm grateful for the support of my students. One took me in for a month; I lived in her backyard guest house. Another held me in her arms and said, "Mellara, I'm worried about you. You're so thin." I was weak and fragile, and looked anorexic. When I was with Ben he would pay for the mortgage and the bigger bills like water and power and I would pay for our food and cover the smaller bills. I thought I could live completely on my own income, but I was shocked to realize that I really wasn't making enough money to pay for rent and everything else. I also hadn't been teaching yoga to that musician for the time that Ben and I were married which was a much more significant cut to my income than I realized. I needed the support of others and I needed to heal and be safe enough in my living environment to stop and feel. I remember feeling old in my bones and weak in my heart. And the grief was overwhelming at times. The loss of my relationship with Ben was so consuming that I couldn't wrap my head around working any harder either. After the month in the backyard guest house, I moved into Oakwood Apartments and began using my credit card for everything extra.

Another yoga student, a woman who owned a massage business, suggested I begin selling myself for sex. She said she hated seeing me this down. "You should be on top, Mellara. You need to carry yourself the way you teach, and not the way I see you now." So she made this offer: "I'll organize for you to meet someone who owns a parlor in Arizona, and you can see if it's right for you and whether you want to go through with it." "Through with what?" I asked, naively. She said the client would want a massage, then he'll want sex. "You're a pure young-looking girl, and you'll make a lot of money. If you go to Arizona a few days a month, you'll make enough to cover your rent. A lot of girls are doing this."

Even though it wasn't what I'd pictured myself doing, I reluctantly agreed and met her at her place of business one evening to "audition" for the position. She had me massage her first to see if I knew what I was doing, and offered some tips. Then an unshaven, balding, overweight man came in. I gave him a massage, and after the hour I stepped out and went to the bathroom. When I came back, he was lying on his back naked, his penis erect. My friend and student explained that he was waiting for me to do something, and I ran out! I couldn't go through with it, whatever was planned.

This was a pattern of mine, like the time I thought I could do a *Playboy* photoshoot. When I was nineteen, I was working at the restaurant and I still remember where I was standing when I was scouted by two photographers for the magazine. It was the side table with the best view overlooking the beautiful people as they would pass on by. With my hair tossed in a light bedroom-looking bun with delicate curls cascading down from my ingénue face, these two *Playboy* photographers were smitten. One of them gave me his card, and said they had just come from a shoot and that I was just what they were looking for. And the whole Australian element made it even more sexy, they said. I called the number on the card and set up a test shoot, arrived at the studio in Beverly Hills, but didn't end up walking in. It just didn't seem right for me at the time.

I felt like a walking contradiction. On one hand I was given aesthetically beautiful looks (I say this not to be boastful but to own it) and unconsciously, I thought this meant my look should be objectified and commodified. Doing this made me into "someone" which was so much more than I ever felt on the inside. And on the other side of the coin, here I was in an adult woman's body still acting from my eight-year-old self who didn't get her needs met—a girl who so desperately wanted to be loved, held emotionally, nurtured, and made to feel safe. Living in Hollywood with other folks vibing with that same energy was a recipe for disaster!

Just the fact that I considered selling my body to men in Arizona showed my level of desperation and lack of self-esteem at the time. I stayed friends with my dear yoga friend. I knew she was only trying to help. I could see the greater good in her, and there was no reason to judge her. In the end, she was one of the only people in my life at the time who was emotionally and physically there for me and accepted me as I was. She was a dedicated yoga student and came religiously to my classes. She would cook the most incredible homecooked meals and treat me like her own child, who was at the time in high school. I loved being at her home. I could be myself. She "got" me and always wanted more for me. I could see that any suggestions she offered were for me, not for her.

She also encouraged me to date again—and never to pay for dinner—if the men weren't generous, I should count them out! At this stage, I only had three sexual partners—the older man I lived with as a teenager, and my two husbands—and I'd never dated around. I only knew to marry; I didn't know how to just have fun.

So I started dating, though I wasn't ready and really needed to heal. I began with two attorneys. When one of them said to me, "Is Mellara ready for her free meal now?" I felt so ashamed, in part because I knew it was true, but still what an asshole! So I never saw him again. I went with the other guy and after we had gone out on a few dates, I blew caution to the wind and had sex with him even though I didn't think it was going to go anywhere. As I look back on it, I just wasn't loving myself enough to say no to what other people wanted, and the attention of someone holding me was what I was looking for the most. I found the whole dating process exhausting.

Then I met John, and I really liked him. He was bubbly like champagne, always knew just what to say, and with what I'd been through I loved that about him. He seemed gentle, kind, and non-judgmental, and he was Catholic. He looked after his elderly parents in the Valley, and I liked that too. He worked hard at his job and made a good living as a salesman. Although we really liked each other, I could see that he wasn't ready to commit to a full-time relationship and that he seemed like he would need a lot more time to decide.

One day while I was teaching at Westlake Yoga, the idea popped into my head that I could make better choices in men if I understood my dad better. So I decided then and there to move back to Australia and give it a try. I was twenty-seven, and my divorce was not yet final. I told my mum, and she snapped at me.

"Stop avoiding the pain, Mellara. Stop running away! Feel it!" Her words were actually wise, but she said it in such a mocking, belittling voice that I shut down. I felt ashamed and couldn't let in what she was saying. I think my mum carried a lot of guilt about me, and she dealt me low blows regularly, words with so much pain wrapped up in the delivery that even her wisest messages couldn't get through.

But I knew that understanding my dad—and through him "the masculine"—could help me in many ways, so I gathered my courage and did it. I put a dozen cartons on a container ship bound for Brisbane, sold my car to hire a divorce lawyer, and purchased plane tickets, leaving me with a few hundred dollars in the bank. Tired of being a magnet for broken partners, I headed home.

CHAPTER THREE

Third Time's the Charm

When I arrived back in Australia, I moved in with Papa and Mammiee, taking care of them in their old age. They were fragile by then, and it turned out to be the last time I had with them before the onset of Mammiee's dementia. She had just overcome bowel cancer, and it was important to me to be there to care for her and help clean house. It was also nice *not* to be teaching twenty yoga classes a week, and instead have only simple, basic tasks. It was a huge about-face from the life I was leading in LA.

My first day back, Papa said to me, "The Crown Prince of Denmark should have chosen *you*." An Australian woman three years older than I had met the Crown Prince at a pub in Sydney, and four years later they were married. It was the biggest news in Australia. Although Papa was probably paying me a compliment—his great-grandfather migrated from Denmark to Australia in the 1860s—I was vulnerable and without resilience, and what I heard was that I'm not good enough as I am.

Around six years later, after I was back in the US, I would visit both my grandparents for the last time in their Mater Prize home, taking with me my third husband Mike and my daughter

Leela, then nine months old. By then, my mum was helping them a lot, and they also had someone coming to bathe Mammiee and help Papa. My son Charlie was born just over two years later, and never got to meet my maternal grandparents.

As my grandmother continued to decline, they moved into an assisted living home, with doctors and nurses present 24/7. Mike and I visited them once more, before Charlie was born. Papa's mind was pretty much intact but Mammiee wasn't responsive. She just laid in bed and didn't do or say much. I told my mum I wanted to remember them the way they were in their beautiful home, and Mum snapped, "Mellara, get real! This is how they are." Once again, my heart was broken. I had always seen my grandparents as strong and never imagined they'd become this fragile. As I look back, there was truth and wisdom in my mum's comment, but I wasn't ready to hear it. I also wanted to feel closer to her as my grandparents were declining, but it just wasn't possible.

Family Matters

After three months at my grandparents' house, I decided to move in with my dad. I was nervous about it because I didn't know how it was going to go, but I knew I needed to try. Just before I did this, Mum moved in to help my grandparents and the tension in the house didn't feel helpful for any of us. My mum made moving in official and went on a caregiver's pension through Centrelink, an Australian government program to help family members in need. It did feel good that she would be there to help them. I think all of us liked that and she was good to them.

My dad and his mum were living in a rundown, government-subsidized home in Nerang, a town and suburb in the city of Gold Coast, Queensland. My paternal grandma was a bully, always calling my dad and me horrible names, and now dementia was setting in. "F-ing American bitch," she shouted at me, saying I didn't sound Australian anymore. She would drink eight or nine bottles of Guinness before 8 p.m., so at least she was passed out by the time I got home from my various jobs and activities. She was right, though. I did sound American and felt more American than Australian. I didn't belong anywhere! The only consistent in my life was feeling unworthy.

It varies from person to person whether they lose their accent when they move to a new place. When I moved to LA, people would often ask me to repeat what I'd said; they couldn't understand my dialect, and I knew I'd never get a break in Hollywood if I couldn't be understood. In acting school, they taught Standard American English. There were many voice exercises, and one was to talk with a wine cork inside your mouth. I would practice for hours both in class and at home, talking around the cork. I so wanted to belong! Today, my Aussie accent is barely noticeable. I worked hard to mask it back then, and it became natural to me to speak "American." I don't need a cork today, but oddly, when I'm deeply relaxed or when I'm teaching, I pronounce some words the Australian way.

When I was little, the few times my paternal grandmother greeted me, she'd bend down to my level and say, "Hello little girl, how beautiful you are," sounding to me like the evil witch who gave Snow White the apple. She had the energy of a cold politician—not caring, no phone calls, no presents, just a lonely woman. When I was small, it felt like rejection. One day when I was little, I went to visit my dad at the caravan park she lived in before she moved into the housing commission home in Nerang. My grandmother would take forever putting on her lipstick, and then when we got in the car to drive to the Returned and Services League (RSL) Club for lunch, it wasn't okay to roll down the windows because her hair would get messy. Gold Coast weather is humid, and it was unbearably stuffy being in that car with the smell of her sprayed hair. But it did stay in place!

As I look back on those years, she seemed empty, anxious, and she was always yelling. My dad has one brother and had one sister who died many years before after giving birth to her son. So in the end it was my dad who was the only one who stayed with their mum till she died. While I was there living with them,

Dad would pick her up when she fell and clean up the feces she left on the bathroom floor without saying a word.

When I was five, Dad's mum owned an apartment building on the Gold Coast and a restaurant in Burleigh Heads. I remember visiting the restaurant with my mum and her parents. Dad worked there as a waiter. Later, Grandma lost the building and the restaurant, in part due to gambling, and ended up in government-assisted housing, living off her RSL benefits.

Despite the chaos of my dad's life and his mother's condition that made it hard to live with them, I was able to establish a routine—morning swims with Dad, teaching yoga twice a week at My Health Yoga in Broadbeach, and even landing an acting gig at Village Roadshow Studios on the Gold Coast, the largest movie studio in Australia. I had the acting bug again. My resumé was strong, and I got a part in a TV movie called *Big Reef*, which was released in 2004.

Swimming in the ocean with my dad, I felt like a kid again and recognized that just because he wasn't a good father, it didn't mean he didn't love me. He loved me in the few ways he could, and I saw that a connection with him was possible. He continued selling drugs though on a much smaller scale from what I could tell. And on some nighttime deliveries I started smoking pot with him; there was plenty around. I actually enjoyed bonding with my dad in those ways. With the car window open, driving and looking out to the moonlight while smelling the fresh air, our conversations were often deeper in nature. He liked talking about world events, his workout goals, and stories about himself and his friends. He also loved having me with him. I think it brought in a gentle energy that at times would balance the intensity he experienced looking after his mother. Spending this time with him I could see that at his core he was a good person who just wasn't given the right conditions to grow to his full potential.

Still, I felt broken all over. The room I stayed in was filthy, and it was, to say the least, humbling to be there. A year earlier, I'd married into a super wealthy family on a Malibu cliffside, and now I was with my down-and-out dad on the outskirts of Southeast Queensland. It ripped away layers of ego, and I was feeling raw. It was horrifying to see what my life had become. I was living not just *with* my parents, but *like* them. I couldn't run away anymore, because wherever I went, my body and mind came with me. I needed to start my journey within myself and practice the spiritual side of yoga. It was a huge wake-up call.

One With the Waves

First and foremost, my dad's a surfer. He says the oneness he feels on the waves helps him through depression. I always picture a 1970s dance video with my dad wearing gold chains around his neck, symbolizing how he allowed wealth—or the lack of it—to strangle him. Money was his everything. It would come in fast and leave just as quickly. When I was little, he never took me shopping, but we did go to the races and I'd help him bet on horses. I believe he had a desire to be more, but he equated love with gold and never had much of either.

His car was old and his furniture decrepit, barely worthy to sit on. But I was grateful to be there, realizing he just didn't know any better. His dad had died when he was ten, and he'd never really been fathered. He looked after his body, though, with lots of supplements and workouts at the gym which he said kept him away from feeling the blues.

In October 2017, eleven years after I had lived with him, I phoned him while I was at the yoga center in Melbourne. We had fallen out of touch because when I came back to America after living with him, I think he expected that I would take care of a friend of ours by sending her money to Australia. She was a yoga friend, and was finding it hard to work because of visa requirements. She was from another country and just scraping by. I could completely relate to her story and wanted to help her. I think my dad had a crush on her too and I was jealous of their relationship and that she was living much closer to him than I was. I ended up sending her some money from the States, but when I stopped doing it I remember him yelling and calling me every name in the book and saying that I was just like my mother.

I was so shaken from the experience that I went no contact for years after that. To be fair it must have been a very stressful time while he was the only caretaker of his mother, but at the time I didn't see it that way at all.

So when I called him that October, he seemed shocked that I had called him and said he had just woken up from taking a nap. Maybe he was nervous that I called him at all, because mostly he went on about this new supplement he loved that made him look and feel younger. It was rather strange for that to be such a big subject because it had been so long since we had spoken, yet it seemed normal too. Not much had changed. He never asked about my beautiful new family—and to this day, he still hasn't physically met Mike, Leela, and Charlie. We have had some wonderful phone calls and it's been good to reconnect after all these years. He seems softer, reformed and curious about me and my life with Mike and the kids. He has also mentioned that if he could do it all over again that he would, and that he's sorry for how things were between us back then, which filled my heart with love and my eyes with tears. Today when I see my dad through clear eyes—without the filter of expectations—I really like his energy. Even though I haven't liked a lot of his choices, especially selling drugs, I know that I love him and my mother and always will. It's this feeling that sits well in my body. What really matters most is love.

Channa was listening to my conversation that day at the studio and suggested that I identify the parts of him that are in me and witness them with great compassion. The way that I move in the world is a direct result of the way my dad did. I made a conscious decision *not* to do what he did, and I can now say that his gift to me was the gift of stability. Because of his erratic lifestyle, I craved stability and found a stable man. I now encourage a stable family life, and offer that to my children.

After living with my maternal grandparents for three months and then my father and his mum for seven, I was ready to head back to Hollywood. I'd bottomed out and began to develop an unalterable relationship with truth. When I told him, my dad said to me, "America has been good for you, and you're still young."

Choiceless Choice

Returning to California was a choiceless choice. I felt I couldn't go any lower than living with my dad who seemed in survival mode, and my mum was not speaking to me. Bottoming out was somehow energizing. After being with my parents, my maternal grandparents, and my dad's mum, I felt that after lots of tears and ocean swims, anything would be okay. I was determined to be more of a grownup and not make choices that made my life worse. Life had beaten me up, and I felt a freshness returning to the States. I loved America. I not only wanted to be here, I needed to be there. I felt both vulnerable and stronger at the same time, shaken but with newfound purpose—to connect deeply with myself and feel whole.

I had just one suitcase and far less emotional baggage. The less I carried, the freer I felt. I wished I'd left Australia as a teenager in 1993 this way. The years of acting, working so many jobs, relationships with the older man, my marriages to Tommy and Ben—it all led to a kind of freedom. Getting to know my dad, I could see his characteristics in me and began to accept my life. My purpose, for the first time, was *to enjoy life*, to have some fun rather than taking myself so seriously. At least that's what I thought as I left Australia to return to the US.

While staying with my grandparents, then with my dad and his mum, I'd kept in touch with John, the nice guy I'd begun dating before leaving LA. I even sent him UGG boots from Down Under when they were still an Australian brand. John bought my plane ticket back to Los Angeles. I was excited to be with him, and I wore a special dress for the fourteen-hour flight so I'd look nice when I arrived. John picked me up at the airport, but didn't seem all that enthused to see me. Still, I was grateful to escape Australia and make it back to California, and I chalked it up to him being tired and told myself it didn't matter anyway. I'd experienced so much pain in Australia, I was ready for a new life. Anything would be better than where I was coming from!

I moved in with John that day and barely left his house till our relationship was over. He was seven years older than I, but he'd never lived with anyone before. He was for sure a late bloomer. I felt supported and loved by him, but something wasn't quite right.

During the time I was with John, my divorce with Ben was finalized, and I was awarded $75,000 plus attorney's fees. Finally, I had some money and could pay off my debts.

As I'd started at my dad's, I continued to smoke pot. My friend Sally, a woman I'd met at Lee Strasberg, smoked with me. We were like sisters and always helped each other during our Hollywood years. While I was with Tommy and then Ben, she lived in Utah. Then she moved back. She was going through a lot in her marriage and we talked about it all while we smoked. John would sit back and drink vodka. Over time, I began to notice he had a problem with drinking and drugs. He was becoming paranoid, imagining people were following him. One afternoon I came home and found him in the shower curled up in the fetal position and crying. I asked what was wrong, but he didn't say much. He always held his cards close to his chest.

On weekends, we would drive from the Valley to Culver City to be with his friends, staying overnight and partying the whole weekend. It was exhausting! I hadn't realized how heavy into the drug scene they all were, especially John. To fit in, one night I did cocaine; I'd never done it before. Then Ecstasy! Sex with John on drugs was horrible, but that's all we wanted to do while we were high. I partied with him and his friends for about a month, then just stopped because I felt so depressed and off-balance. Doing drugs wasn't me at all. If it had been, I would have started a lot earlier.

During my time with John, I didn't look for another place or another partner, because I felt safe with him. He was another man who was beautiful and kind inside, and made some bad choices—getting into drugs, probably to escape his pain. Finally I left him. I feel fortunate to have had the time I did with John. I loved him, but finally accepted he wasn't the right person for me.

Health and Longevity

After returning to LA with lots of lessons learned, and a brief interlude continuing under my old assumptions—that I needed a man to take care of me, that distraction and denial served me, and that I had no needs of my own—at the age of twenty-nine, I was determined to begin life anew, to live more consciously, and to stop being drawn to the magnet of the destructive patterns I knew too well.

After I left John, I rented a room in a huge private home in Westlake Village near the yoga studio. My idea was that I'd be content with just a roof over my head and the simple fruits and vegetables I could buy at the farmers market. The yoga studio owner at Westlake Village, who was always loving and support-ive, gave me all my classes back. I had called her from Australia, and she said, "Just come back and we'll make it work."

A few months after I started teaching again, I was contacted by a wealthy businessman who asked if I would teach him yoga, and I said yes. At first, I taught him as I would teach anyone, with an open heart and focused energy. I noticed that he was taking an interest in me, and I did have a curiosity about him too. He was decades older than me, and I found myself reminiscing about those times in the car with my mum's older boyfriend, Don, and the way we sang show tunes together.

He was a kind and sweet man and at the same time something of a rascal—exactly my type! The strange-attractor magnet in me was still strong, despite my efforts to turn over a new leaf. The yoga lessons and breakfasts, his flirtations and incessant efforts to widen the boundaries of our relationship, and my continued wish to have a father-lover figure in my life characterized our time together. He started to give me lots of money from his safe, hundreds of dollars, because he said that he wanted me to get some nice clothes for myself. His only condition was that I couldn't save it. I bought a lot of clothes with his money, saved some and bought an iPod. I could see that he was falling in love with me and one day as he leaned in for a kiss goodbye (on the cheek) he moved me over to the couch with his hands on my hips and started to kiss me on the lips while embracing me. Everything happened so quickly and I felt startled by it all, yet not surprised. I just didn't have it in my mind that we would be lovers. Later I thought that I was probably a big tease to him, but I didn't see a long-term future, and I felt I needed to be with someone more my own age. So I got up and said, "Sorry, this isn't for me" and picked up my things and never saw him again.

Years later, he crossed my mind again. Finally I was able to see my part and how I had caused him pain and not just the other way around. After experiencing Channa's teachings, I was able to witness myself as a confused little girl, and I could open the space around my heart and embrace her. I felt a rush of lightness and was able to forgive myself and him too. Sometimes realities that are swept under the rug because of the pain they cause re-arise. Channa told me, "We don't need more information. We need to let things be as they are. That's what brings us home."

"I Love You, Too"

After a three-month on-again, off-again flirtation with the older businessman, I told myself I would have to be okay even if I never married again or had children. I was looking for acceptance and healing, to be okay with myself regardless of whether I was in a relationship.

Not long after, Mike, who is now my husband and the father of our two beautiful children, came into the studio in Westlake Village and signed up for private yoga lessons to heal from arrhythmia. Mike was easy on the eye: tall, handsome, clean-cut, with brown hair. He had a gentle heart, kind eyes, and an intellectual mind, yet he also seemed like an outdoorsy person too.

I began the first session teaching him to meditate. Maybe four minutes in, I opened my eyes and looked at him as if to say, "Did you feel that?" His eyes were closed, so I didn't say anything. But I'd never had a feeling like that before. The only way I can describe it is a profound sense of oneness, a deep soul connection, not romantic or lustful. I felt like I'd known him before, or that I was becoming acquainted with someone who would be very special in my life. At that point, after all my experiences, I didn't trust myself to open up. And so even with my strong feelings, I remained professional.

I consulted a Vedic astrologer, and asked whether Mike was going to be abusive. That's all I wanted to know. The astrologer assured me that Mike didn't have an abusive chord in his chart and that I'd be safe with him. I loved having that information.

I continued teaching, giving no hint that revealed my feelings. Months passed, and one day he walked in as usual, sat down, and looked ready for his lesson. But he also looked like he had something to share. "Mellara," he said, "I'm going to say something that might keep me from continuing class." He looked worried, yet determined. I said, "If there's anything you'd like to say, please feel free. You're safe here."

He said, "I love you," and without hesitation I replied, "I love you, too." It was beautiful and a relief, because I'd felt the same but was never going to express it given that I was the teacher and had learned so many painful lessons. We remained in our seated meditation positions for a while, just smiling. Mike is usually reserved, and only people closest to him get to see his warmth and humor. He has a disciplined, Zen-like energy that can be misread by people who don't know him well. It was huge for him to say something like that, and I knew it came from the depths of his soul, a true expression of his heart.

After that, I was no longer Mike's teacher. The roles changed, not formally, but now he teaches me more about myself when I remain open to the connection of love that brought us together.

As our relationship progressed, we began to talk about marriage only a few months into it. It probably seemed quick from the outside, yet we had both been married before and knew we wanted to start a family as soon as we could. I think deep down we finally knew we had found "the one." I asked the Vedic astrologer to help us find the most auspicious time and place for our marriage. In India, they've been deciding special dates through Vedic astrology since the dawn of time. I'm not sure

Mike believed an astrologer could know these kinds of things, but he was really open to me and appreciated the different colors I brought to our union. We married at the water's edge in Burleigh Heads on the Gold Coast on January 1, 2007. I'm forever grateful for our union, and though it's not perfect—just like me and all of us—it's a love that continues to grow deeper and wider than my mind can fathom.

Although we had an instant connection beyond anything either of us had felt before, I still experienced myself as damaged goods, unworthy. I still needed healing and balance, and I was ready to be taken care of by Mike and start a family together.

Six months after the wedding, our daughter Leela was born. We named her after the Sanskrit word which translates into sacred play. Later, at a retreat with Channa in Bali, I was so moved by these words he spoke in a video he created, which he's allowed me to use here.

It's happening everywhere at every moment
Be still
Notice the observer and the observed

Look at the flower
You might have a botanical analysis
But you won't experience its essence

Without saying anything allow the blossom to merge with you,
So you're not there and it's not there
Beautiful intimacy.

Innocence is when you no longer act from the mind
There's a purity
You don't experience from memory but as it is in this moment.

Just be
Experience everything without being there
And only the experience is left

This is Leela
A dance
A trance

PART TWO

Entering the Practice

*Moments after we met, he asked, "Why are you here?" I repeated
the question inside myself, Why am I here? Does he mean
Melbourne or earth? After a pause that felt like forever,
he clarified, "What have you come to do in this life?"*

CHAPTER FOUR

Deep Healing

Mike's workplace had massive layoffs. The job market in Westlake and Thousand Oaks wasn't good at the time, and Mike didn't want a long commute to LA from Westlake. So we decided to move to San Francisco, where Mike already owned an apartment, and he got a job with a bank there. I loved the idea of moving out of the suburbs into a city! Leela was six weeks old when we drove north in two cars, Mike by himself and me with Leela in an infant carrier in the back seat.

Mike's apartment was a second-floor walkup that had a landing halfway up the stairs. We had a tandem parking spot that we shared with a man who lived in the apartment above us, so to take my car out, I often had to move his car first. Baby carriages are lighter than they used to be, but they're still heavy, and to go shopping—or anywhere by car—I had to leave Leela in the apartment, move our neighbor's car, park my car on the street, put his car back, walk back to the apartment, and bring Leela, her stroller, and car seat back down the stairs. Leela was colicky and never slept through the night her first year. Mike did what he could to help, but with the new job, he worked long hours. I was exhausted from being a new mom, suffered from postpartum depression, and didn't know anyone in San Francisco to ask for help.

One time when Leela and I got back from the market, I left her in the car to carry the groceries up to the landing. As I ran back down the stairs to get her, our neighbor started yelling that I was abusive, leaving our precious little girl in the car alone. I'd never lost sight of her, but I knew the neighbor was right. I was deeply depressed the rest of the day. Abusing Leela was the last thing I ever wanted to do. My own childhood flashed before my eyes.

Mike tried to be helpful when I was depressed. "You seem sad, Mellara. Where is my young and beautiful wife?" He had no idea that saying that made me feel even worse, as though I had it in my power to just start feeling better. I wasn't taking care of my appearance, and Mike could see that I was out of sorts. Thanks to his efforts, I came to admit something was wrong, but it was hard to shake this feeling. Later, working with Channa, I would realize I needed to stop *trying* to get out of the feeling and just experience it in order to begin healing.

Mike tried to help me see when I was caught by the role of victim. He'd say, "It's okay to visit Pity City, but you don't want to live there." He'd heard that from a motivational speaker. I didn't realize it at the time, but I wanted him to feel sorry for me. I had no clue that what I needed was my own love and sense of worth. I thought it was easy for him to say, because he just left and went to work every day while I was left at home with Leela—and without him. Rather than feeling supported, which was his intention, I felt abandoned again.

I got jealous when he went out for business dinners with colleagues, including some women, even though nothing was going on. I conjured it all in my mind to reinforce the victim role, that the world was against me. I felt alone, depressed, and petty. During those first two years with Mike in San Francisco while I was a new mother, I recognized that I'm with a caring man, true to his word, a "steady Eddie." I married the very nurturance and trustworthiness I'd never received—an honest partner—and lived in a stable home where I felt safe to grow mentally, spiritually, and physically, but it was difficult to let it all in.

One morning, Mike left a note on the kitchen table:

My love has eyes that
See goodness and a
Smile that brings joy.

My love speaks a truth
That can only come
From the heart.

My love has strength
Through love and
Life and loss.

My love radiates the
Divine from within
And without, to all.

My love is
Mellara!

To be continued!

Mike was and is *so* supportive. Over time I became more skillful at shopping for groceries, mothering Leela, and dealing with parking. I stopped using our parking space and just parked on the street. And mostly I walked, which was great exercise, and Leela and I enjoyed the city together. We'd leave the apartment around nine o'clock and I'd push her in her carriage all over Cow Hollow, the Marina, the Presidio, and further. Even on freezing days, we loved going to the beach! The city was refreshing, and it was fun to be around shops and of course the Palace of Fine Arts and Crissy Field.

I'd put our fruits, veggies, and milk inside the stroller. The stores in our neighborhood were expensive, but it was easier than dealing with the car. I lost a lot of my child-bearing weight walking the hills of San Francisco. And I joined the fitness program at the Presidio YMCA, where I met Suzy Dito. Instantly she felt like family.

Doldrums

When I met Suzy at the YMCA, she was the human resources manager there. Leela was three months old, old enough to stay in childcare. Not only did I work out at the Y, but Suzy gave me my first yoga teaching job in San Francisco. The group exercise manager wasn't convinced I was a good fit, but Suzy disagreed and gave me a shot, something she told me many years later. Suzy was a yoga teacher at the Y too, and she also ended up coming to my classes. Later, when we left San Francisco to move to Melbourne, she was the only person who helped us. She even stayed with the kids and me on our last night to help us finish packing in time for the moving people. I couldn't have done it without her. And later, too, she became my colleague, helping to organize Channa's US retreats.

I applied for teaching jobs at other yoga studios too, but even with my experience, there seemed to be a disconnect between how yoga was taught in Northern versus Southern California. One studio owner told me I should come to their classes "to see how we teach here." Even though I had a strong resumé, it seemed to mean nothing. So once again, I felt rejected, as I'd felt as a child when we moved so often. The yoga world was something I thought I could count on, and I'm sure this added to my depression.

I ended up teaching at the Presidio YMCA every Saturday and eventually every other Saturday for nearly six years. After we moved to the East Bay, our whole family would commute to the city on Saturdays. It had a beautiful energy. Mike enjoyed an excuse to be in the city, and he and the kids had a great time, or sometimes he'd put them in childcare and go for a long walk, which he loved.

Despite all the positives, depression continued to be my default. Before we left LA, Mike and his team at work took personality tests to help management understand how each person makes decisions. The project administrator at Mike's company allowed me to take the test too. It showed that I was both introverted and extraverted. The administrator said this is sometimes the test result when an extravert is depressed. At the time, we just shrugged our shoulders, but now I see he was probably right. Even though I'd found a place to settle with a loving husband and a beautiful baby girl, I still needed to dive more deeply inward. Fortunately, that was coming soon.

Warmth

Mark Twain is quoted as saying, "The coldest winter I ever spent was a summer in San Francisco." The longer we lived in San Francisco, the more the damp cold seeped through to my bones and discs, and I began wearing a heating pad on my lower back. By the time I was pregnant with Charlie, I was ready to move somewhere warmer, with simpler logistics. Being raised in Queensland and spending fourteen years in LA, I missed the warm weather.

So, two years after moving to San Francisco, we started looking for a house, first in Marin County across the Golden Gate Bridge, then in the San Francisco Peninsula south of the city, and finally in the valleys east of the Berkeley hills. Summers there are quite hot, which appealed to me. We found a home in the East Bay, a place where I could come and go easily with the kiddos, and Mike had an easy commute to work. The school district was highly rated and shopping was a breeze. Mike could have stayed in the city longer, but he agreed to move.

By the time we relocated, few symptoms of depression remained, and I was ready to be active again. We enrolled Leela in preschool, where it turned out the movement teacher was about to leave her job. For me to apply for her position, I needed to earn twelve early-childhood education credits.

Every morning, while Leela was at preschool, I took Charlie with me to the gym. But instead of working out, I'd sit in the gym's café and study, and was able to complete an online program and get the credits I needed, a huge accomplishment for me. Later, we qualified for a faculty tuition discount at the same preschool for Charlie.

At first, I was excited to be teaching movement to kids. I developed a yoga program for three-to-seven-year-olds and offered lots of other movement exercises. But after two years of teaching children, I started to feel depressed again. I couldn't work anymore. The kids being kids seemed loud and needy; but as I look back on this today, this is how I was feeling about myself and it really wasn't about the kids at all. My head was spinning with the usual kinds of self-defeating voices and pity I knew all too well. Looking out the window onto beautiful Mt. Diablo, I thought, "Please God, place me in an environment that works for me. It's not with these beautiful children anymore. Please allow my life to change in ways that are right for me and my family." Little did I realize I would soon meet my teacher Channa.

Under the supervision of a doctor, I began taking antidepressants without telling Mike for nearly a month. I didn't want to worry him. When I finally told him, he offered his support for me to leave my job and rest. I quit, stopped taking meds, and began to feel much better.

I went back to working out at the gym and practicing yoga, Pilates, and more. Doing this always keeps me balanced. I also decided to have surgery for the ab separation I'd developed with two nine-pound births. I needed my stomach muscles to come back together to support the pain in my lower back. But something was still missing—a connection to myself.

Ready

Although she was born in California, Leela is Australian "by descent." When she began first grade in 2013. she spotted a classmate eating the famous Aussie food spread Vegemite, and told me I *had* to meet her new friend's mom, Miriam. The family had just moved back to the Bay Area after four years of living in Melbourne.

Miriam and I became fast friends. She kept telling me how beautiful her life was in Melbourne, especially her yoga practice with a teacher named Channa Dassanayaka. I was moved by her devotion, not just the way she talked about Channa, but that she'd soon be flying *thirty hours* to Bali to attend a retreat with him. Miriam began attending my yoga classes, and I observed her deep connection to meditation and especially her unwavering lotus posture. I was curious to learn more about her practice.

A few months later, Miriam sent me a YouTube link* with a brief message: "This is my teacher and the community in Australia. I hope we can visit them together." As I lay in a warm bath watching the clip on my iPhone, my heart nearly pounded out of my chest. I *had* to go there to learn from this remarkable teacher and cultivate the grace and beauty, the acceptance, love, and magic that I felt while watching the video. I sent a prayer out to the universe that if I was meant to be a part of this center, I was ready! My soul was yearning for an experience like that.

During my birthday dinner in October 2014, Mike suggested that when we visit my family in Queensland the following year, we also take a vacation in Melbourne. Growing up on the eastern side of Australia, I only heard about Melbourne as a vibrant, creative city, but I'd never been there. Mike was working for an international software firm, so I said, "Honey, why don't you see if your company has an opening in Melbourne? Maybe we could move there." He agreed, and I remember feeling so grateful for his support. He even seemed excited about the idea. Mike and I don't always see things the same way, yet in that moment I had an *Aha!* moment. I recognized that he's an incredible life partner who shares my adventurous spirit.

Lo and behold, there *was* a position in Melbourne, similar to the one he held in San Francisco, and within a couple of weeks he completed the interviews, got the job, and we were preparing

---

* https://youtu.be/zLN2xG-eBZI

to move! We had only seven weeks to rent out our home in the Bay Area and get our things onto a container ship. Mike flew down early to begin work and find us a home to rent, and I stayed back with the kids to pack up the house. The company Down Under had been looking for months for someone to fill this position and were thrilled to get an experienced data-analytics guy from California. Seven years earlier we had obtained a Partner Visa, not knowing whether we'd ever use it. Now, having that visa allowed Mike to accept the job. In a very short time, Leela, now seven, Charlie, five, and I were ready to join Mike in Melbourne.

Hours before our departure, Miriam dropped by with gifts, including a copy of Channa's cookbook, *Sri Lankan Flavours: A Journey Through the Island's Food and Culture*, and a tiny cosmetic bag that had a map of Melbourne on the side. She said I should ask Channa to sign the book for me. She also told me that as she was leaving Australia, Channa had said she would bring someone to him, and she was certain it was me. Hearing her words sent chills up my spine, and if I wasn't excited enough for this adventure, now I was even more eager to meet her teacher! I'm so grateful to Miriam for all her help navigating our international move and connecting me with the Dassanakaya Yoga community.

Down Under

Although transitioning to this new life brought our family closer together, it wasn't easy. There was a shipping strike in California, and the container with our belongings took five months to arrive. We had to manage with the one suitcase we brought with us, and bought everything else essential in Melbourne—beds, kitchen appliances, and other things as needed.

Arriving in Melbourne was both exhilarating and depressing. I loved being Down Under, feeling the creative, vibrant energy of Melbourne and the anticipation of meeting Channa. But I still felt a fundamental dis-ease. Something was still missing from my life.

Mike didn't have enough time to find a house before we arrived. In Australia, rental property viewings are a group fifteen-minute open house, so Mike was running from house to house as they were all scheduled around the same time. He ran for miles, and got used to the great public transportation, but still came up empty. So his company put us up in corporate housing for two weeks while we got our references and paperwork to secure a home to rent. Even though I hadn't met Channa yet, I wanted a place near his yoga studio, which was an inner suburb six km (3.5 miles) north-east of Melbourne's Central Business District. I imagined I'd spend a fair amount of time there. Mike wanted to live near the sea and his workplace, and we were lucky to find the perfect compromise—a place in the town of Caulfield South, fourteen km (8.6 miles) from the City Center and four miles from the ocean, where sea breezes that salved my soul rolled in every morning and evening. We were however eighteen km away from Channa's studio, about eleven miles from us, and what I didn't know then was that Melbourne traffic can be quite challenging in the peak hours.

In California, we owned a middle-class suburban home. The kids had their own rooms, their own play area, and a half-acre of grassy backyard. The Bay Area's cost of living is high, but Melbourne's is off the charts! We rented a two-and-a-half-bedroom townhome, where the kids shared one bedroom, and Mike converted the "half-room" into a yoga and Pilates studio for us. It had no closet, just enough space to move around. No more gardener or cleaning help, and no grassy backyard, just concrete, potted plants, and an Aussie clothesline. Adjusting to this new normal gave us perspective.

Melbourne was voted the most livable city in the world eight years in a row by *The Economist*. Its vibrancy and natural beauty with lots of parks and our lovely house near the sea were great resources during our trials adjusting to such a different life. Once the container ship arrived, we didn't have room for our belongings. So we filled our garage with the extra stuff, and I didn't see most of it until we returned to the US. In fact, I never missed any of it and learned how little we actually need.

Near our house were two public schools for kids Leela and Charlie's ages—the lovely Caulfield South Primary, less than a mile away, and Caulfield Primary, a Japanese immersion school closer to the hustle and bustle of trams, shops, and the main drag. Our address, it turned out, was just outside the district for Caulfield South Primary, and so Leela and Charlie were automatically enrolled in the Japanese school. When I told Mike, he just smiled, surprised but not fazed. He had worked in Japan when he was in his twenties. I was excited for the kids, because I'd read that cognitive health is nurtured by immersion in a second language. When I told Leela, she nearly fell over in amazement and a touch of horror. I don't think she believed me.

Not only had we brought our American kids to a new country, now they'd be attending a Japanese-immersion school, speaking only Japanese fifteen hours a week, including in math, art, performing arts, and science classes. Only English and physical education were taught in English. When I saw Leela after her first day of school, her eyes spoke volumes. She paused, looked at me directly, placed her two feet firmly on the ground, and with huge eyes and a lot of sass, said, "Mom, the whole day was in Japanese. How on earth is this going to work?" She had a good grasp on things and was great at communicating when something didn't appeal to her. She's heartfelt and has her dad's straight-shooting nature. I took a deep breath and said, "Sweetheart, you're one of the smartest, kindest people I know. I'm sure you'll find your way through it." Inside, I was a little less convinced.

Once we settled in a bit, it was fun to pick the kids up from school and go to the local bakery, where we got to enjoy cherry slices, croissants that could have been made in France, Aussie meat pies, and sausage rolls. That was our afternoon ritual, and I found it healing to experience my country in a new, redemptive way. We found a crystal shop that sold spiritual books and offered me free cappuccinos and the children hot chocolates while we browsed the books and knickknacks. Melbourne is known for their great coffee and open-hearted folks.

By the end of our first year in Melbourne, the children were thriving. Leela was her class's student council representative. Charlie was footy crazy, an Australian contact sport. Every Monday afternoon, there was a half-hour assembly the parents could attend. *Advance Australia Fair*, the national anthem, was played at the beginning, and all of us were encouraged to sing along. I flashed to my childhood and became quite emotional as I sang the words, "For those who've come across the seas, we've boundless plains to share." I'd been born an Aussie, ran away in anger and confusion as a teen, and moved back twenty years later. I was becoming reacquainted with the land where my soul chose to take human birth, and the tears felt healing, as though I was welcomed back to a place that had never actually shut me out. I hadn't run away from Australia, but from myself. Australia was always ready to hold me in her arms and share her boundless plains.

Healing

A month after we arrived in Melbourne, on February 11, 2015, I visited the Dassanayaka Yoga Centre, Channa's studio. Three weeks earlier, Miriam had sent an email to Channa and me, cc'ing Miriam's close women friends, with the heading, "Something special is about to happen," introducing us to one another. The women got in touch, but I never heard from Channa, so I decided to go without an appointment. Later, after we leased a car, I was able to drive to the center in under an hour, but that day I traveled by train, tram, and taxi, and it took two-and-a-half hours, which was mostly because I got lost on the train and didn't get off of the correct stop so I had to backtrack quite a bit. New friends told me later that it would be best to use a car to get from Caulfield South to the inner city suburbs because it would shave off at least thirty-five minutes of commute time. That first day of meeting Channa felt like the last leg of a pilgrimage, and I took the time en route to reflect on my life.

Suddenly, while I was on the tram, a girl riding a bicycle got her wheels stuck in the tracks right in front of us. She fell and hit her head and was lying there on the ground, as the tram stopped in time and didn't hit her. She was in a lot of pain, and we were all running around trying to help. I held her hand and told her she was going to be okay. Then an ambulance arrived, and we were sent on our way. This was on the day I was going to Channa for healing.

I caught a taxi, and finally arrived at 58 Bastings Street, Northcote. It's a suburban street with beautiful Victorian houses, native plants abundantly on display, mothers pushing prams (baby carriages), and older residents tugging their vegetable carts home after their morning shopping. Many years ago, 58 Bastings had been the local milk bar—a general store and café. Before opening the latch to the front gate, I smelled wafts of incense ready to provide comfort at my time of need. Alongside the gate, a statue of an armored medieval guard was standing upright, representing to me the safety and courage I'd need as I entered the gates of reconnection to my own spirit and wellness. Fragrant potted plants hung beautifully in the morning light. I slowed down to enjoy these gifts before entering.

I removed my shoes. There was a bowl of water there, more a planter than a religious font, but I was moved to place a drop on my forehead. It was probably my Catholic upbringing. Then I rang the bell. Channa, with his partner Darren close behind, answered the door, both of them wearing tank tops and shorts. Not what I expected them to be wearing, but I chalked it up to the heat—Melbourne is so hot in the summer. February is still very hot in Melbourne and it doesn't cool down until March or April. They invited me in and immediately showed me around. I didn't expect to be taken on a tour around their home within our first meeting, or maybe at all, but I slowly remembered that this is what we Australians do. In my childhood, we would always give guests the "grand tour" of my grandparents' home. Australians are friendly and open like that.

It was like a museum, each room filled with artifacts from another time, honored with care and devotion. I noticed a print of a famous old painting of a little girl's face and it was the same one my grandparents had at their home. I was kind of shocked to see it here, and took it as a sign that I was in the right place at the right time. I was also realizing how important beauty is for my spirit. The ambience penetrated my soul, and I began to weep. I felt I had come home.

After a few minutes, Channa began to chant in Pali, the language of the Buddha's early teachings. His voice sounded heavenly to me. Chills or "truth bumps" as I like to call them wouldn't stop coming and my skin felt constantly raised up as I was taken to the depths of my soul. The sound was harmonic almost like many different sounds were being offered at the same time, yet there was only one Channa standing there.

Even before finishing his chant, Channa told me that Mike and I wouldn't be in Australia permanently, that I'd be needed in America in about two years and that Mike would transfer back so it could happen. Imagine hearing this right after our huge international move—closing accounts, shutting everything down, and getting the kids into a new school! Channa didn't even know I'd be coming that day or meeting him at all. There had only been the one unanswered email from Miriam. As a kind of consolation, Channa added that our children would be grateful for the experience of living in Australia. Even still, this news, if true, was hard to let in. Mike and I hadn't decided how long we wanted to stay, but we'd packed up everything to keep our options open.

I couldn't understand what was happening. Then Channa gave me a healing, placing mala beads (prayer beads) over my head, beads I still wear today. He told me I may feel wounded—quite the understatement!—but that everything would be okay. He was in a kind of trance when he asked, "Why are you here?" I repeated the question inside myself, *Why am I here?* Does he mean Melbourne or earth? After a pause that felt like forever, he clarified, "What have you come to do in this life?" *What a question to ask someone minutes after meeting them!* I felt overwhelmed and so much more, just being there. After a few more seconds that again felt like hours, I replied, "I think I'm here to help heal people." Looking back, I believe he was trying to see if I understood my life's purpose so he could correlate what I said with what his guides were telling him. I'd never seen anything like it before, especially his trance state.

Channa went on to tell me I would help deliver the medicines of yoga and awareness to many people and that I was "a mother to all." He's incredibly intuitive, and throughout my time with him, I've come to understand how helpful this is in nurturing and healing people. I'm grateful he told me all that he did, because it encouraged me to focus on his teachings and refrain from exploring my new surroundings as much as I'd planned.

I sat down for a cup of tea, and Barbara, who'd been copied on the email Miriam sent, arrived. I had told her I would try to visit the center that day. Barbara was nurturing and kind, like an old friend even though I was meeting her for the first time. She was a pretty lady, similar in age to me, with short bobbed blonde hair, and a calming Aussie voice. She also seemed proper or "well to do" as my grandparents might say. She was well put together and her clothes, although casual for Melbourne seemed like good quality, stitched well and boutique looking. Melbourne women are known for celebrating individuality and locals seem to wear fashion-forward looks year round, and Barbara was no exception. She stopped by to make sure I arrived okay, and afterward, she drove me to the nearby station where I caught the train back to Caulfield and picked the kids up from school.

I continued to visit the Dassanayaka Yoga Centre to attend classes. After a few weeks, Channa asked if I was a writer. I told him I'd written some little poetry things when I was little and how fun it was to give them to my grandparents, and that I enjoyed that very much, but it wasn't something I did regularly and not something I saw on the horizon. He told me that the time had come, that I would write a book, and he asked me to record his teachings and if anything came to me along the way, to write it down, that I would be guided in the process. Thus, the book you hold in your hands began its journey into the world. Looking back, I see that even though our move to Australia was in part for my reconciliation with the land of my birth and a work opportunity for Mike, it was primarily so I could meet Channa, experience his teachings, and heal on the deepest levels.

Time Out

After we leased a car, I began commuting to the Dassanayaka Yoga Centre three times a week. One day, Channa was talking to another student about how deep the classes were, and I felt it was a push for me to be there more. So I started going to the center four days a week. While I was away from home, nothing got done, so I had to wake up early to do some housework and write chapters of this book if I was going to be with Channa all day. Weekends were family time; I never went to the yoga center on weekends, with one exception—the High Tea fundraiser—which I'll describe later.

By the end of our first year in Melbourne, I was staying at the center longer and longer, just to be around Channa. Darren was always with us too. I helped out however I could, yet it was I receiving the help as I soaked in Channa's teachings and the practices. My teacher and I would water the garden, drink tea, clean the yoga studio, arrange flowers in the shrine, cook, and through it all, he taught me how important it was to be devotional and to make things beautiful for everyday living. I knew how to set a table, but the way Channa did it was kind of the way my grandmother would do for Christmas or other special occasions. The table had the feeling of a Victorian-era dinner party where the values of a refined society were on display, and although no one seemed stuffy or pompous, there was an emphasis on etiquette and proper conduct.

Channa was laying the foundation for me to feel the teachings within the depth of everyday life, to live in awareness, and to celebrate life daily by not waiting for a special occasion to do so. My time with Channa quickly became invaluable. How fortunate I was to receive these spiritual gifts, including the time to heal. I would stay at the center most of each day until it was time to pick the kids up from school. Leela was in grade two, and Charlie was in prep, a compulsory first year of school for Australian children prior to year one (first grade).

Before meeting Channa, I felt unworthy most of the time. As a mom, I had to fortify my children's self-esteem while building up my own. When I got upset with them, I focused on what they had *done* rather than how naughty they *were*, because they weren't. But until becoming Channa's student, I didn't feel whole within and I'd run away inside every time I got angry. It was I who needed time-outs, or in actuality "time-ins" and not my kids. Today I see that *witnessing* is more effective than rules. I spanked my kids a few times before realizing the pain I was delivering was toward myself, repeating patterns of my own conditioning. I remembered how terrible it was to feel that kind of fear for little things, like not eating my dinner or doing something I'd been asked not to. Now, living in awareness, I never fail to tell my children I love them, and in this field of love to encourage them to find their own way.

Chapter Five

The Teachings

One day in class, Channa taught about forgiveness, and in that moment, I could see how easily I fall into the victim role to justify not moving forward. I made demands on my mother, as all children do. We want our parents to be perfect. Now I'm learning to mother as best I can, which is imperfect.

During the time I'd lived in Australia when I was twenty-seven, instead of getting closer with my mum, our relationship became even more strained. I didn't speak with her much, as she seemed too hurt that I had chosen to live with my dad. She basically disowned me, then freaked out when I decided to move back to the States after only ten months.

After meeting Channa, I began to see that this heaviness in the cells of my being never went away. I just covered up my true energy with a pleasant personality and never examined whether others, including my mum, were suffering as I was. I gravitated to those who believed and encouraged my negative stories, reinforcing my feeling of being trapped. I tried to think my way out of my feelings instead of observing and accepting them. I practiced postural yoga to find relief from back pain and emotional stress, without addressing the root causes. Now, under Channa's guidance, I began to live in awareness and connect with the innocence we're all born with, rather than dwell in the conditioning that keeps us imprisoned.

After years of feeling deeply unsettled, being with Channa woke me up, and every feeling, taste, touch, and sound became part of a life worth living. I came to realize that although yoga and other practices are important, they're elements of a larger picture of growth and healing. As I stopped sleeping my life away and began feeling at home inside myself, my inner tensions felt bigger, not smaller. It's not that the anxiety was growing but that I was becoming aware of it. And as I brought awareness to areas that needed more breath, acceptance, and love, my back pain lessened. Stress still arrives regularly, but I've learned to witness it and not be subjected to its stories. A shedding of parts of me that were never really mine began during my days at the center with Channa.

In the past, when pain and emotions would come knocking on my door, I'd blame myself and fret that I was paying too much attention to them or not enough. Now, when these visitors come, I hold them gently and witness them with kindness. I'm able to care for these mind states as they arise. I rarely get angry *at anger* for interrupting the flow of the moment, because when anger arrives, it *is* the moment, and healthy anger has its place in our lives. I know that all mind states warrant compassion, not denial or neglect, and with this attitude, cultivated through practice, I have the chance of making a different choice at the fork in the road. Taking care of myself is now an option.

Channa encourages us to answer the door when emotional visitors knock. The practice is not to disregard their importance while, at the same time, not to *identify* with them or make them bigger. We care primarily for our *beingness.* I no longer put anyone on hold because their arrival inconveniences my schedule. I acknowledge all visitors, witness their presence, and usually that's enough for them to deliver their message and be on their way. Emotions show up all the time. When I'm gentle with myself and deeply present in the moment, I don't feel overwhelmed. I just witness and love each visitor as they arrive.

Thanks to what I learned from Channa, I see that the karmic fruits I experience are not just the results of my personal actions. Everything is the result of multiple causes and conditions and all we can do is pay attention, witness, and respond from the heart. Once the train of deeper consciousness has left the station, there's no turning back. Happiness does not depend on vacations or shopping or bingeing, but on being true to ourselves. Channa has helped me recognize that what I seek is always within.

Café

In Melbourne, people enjoy breakfast all day long. After classes at the center, Channa, Darren, and a few community members would often walk to the Red Door, a colorful, hole-in-the-wall café just a few minutes from the yoga studio. One day at the café, Channa invited us to look at the flower in the center of the table and asked what we saw. One student said, "Beauty, pure beauty." Another said, "It has just a few more days to live." Another observed that one of its buds had not yet opened.

Channa asked us to look more deeply, and as we sat in silence gazing at the flower, a student said, "I see myself in the flower." "Good, you're getting there," Channa encouraged him. "We're no different from the flower, and we can use this insight to liberate ourselves in each moment." I asked why I'd feel liberated about dying, and he explained that it's not impermanence that makes us suffer, it's wanting things to stay the same. "We suffer when we want the moment to be something it isn't. I want to keep this house or this job or this flower forever. I want things to say as they are. Even when the moment isn't comfortable, it's the way it is. We suffer much less when we simply remain present without trying to control the way things are."

If it weren't for impermanence, I wouldn't be able to improve myself or heal, and neither would our precious earth. Being kind to ourselves and others, we can be a part of the change we wish to see in the world. Only change remains constant, and the flower in the café helped me realize that we can live fully in each moment, accepting that the flower—and we—will perish at some point. Because of impermanence, I now give my full attention to loved ones. I don't do it out of fear, but because being present fills the universe with love. Since receiving this teaching on impermanence, I see that even the smallest movements can open our consciousness and that deepening the world's consciousness—one person at a time—is how peace and stability come about.

Over time, visiting the center, listening to Channa's teachings, meditating, and having discussions with other students, I became aware of my spirit inside and being in my truth. Living in awareness, I moved into a deeper acceptance of myself and all that I am, an acceptance that brings me to wholeness. It has nothing to do with religion or even happiness, but is about living the truth of who we really are. This is the moment when healing takes place.

I was witnessing this in the way my playful energy was larger than life at home. Most days after picking up Leela and Charlie at school, we would often go straight to Princes Park which was just a few steps from our home. It is one of Glen Eira's most popular parks, with multiple sportsgrounds, vast open spaces, and significant play spaces that provide opportunities for togetherness, exercise, and relaxation. It felt so spacious to be there, and it mirrored how I was feeling inside. Leela would bring Dolly, a little red-haired stuffed doll that I had picked up for her in San Francisco when I thought Leela might end up having red hair instead of the strawberry blonde that it is today. Charlie would bring his stuffed animal bunny that he loved so much and we would play for what seemed like hours. It was as if time stopped and we were magically given more hours in the day. I also noticed I was much more patient with myself, and I looked so much less at my iPhone as we enjoyed the great outdoors. Back in California we were outside a ton, but the pace and energy was completely different in Melbourne as I became more settled inside.

Each Situation Has Its Own Energy

For many years, Channa had been leading retreats in Bali twice a year. He found the atmosphere at the center there deeply conducive to personal and spiritual growth. One year when a retreat was scheduled, the island's volcano was erupting and the retreat had to be cancelled. As I was filling out the travel insurance claim, I told Channa it would take the insurance company a long time to issue the check. I'd experienced this kind of thing before. I explained that there would have to be an investigation and a lot of questioning. Channa said that wouldn't be the case, that every situation is guided by its own energy and if we skew the outcome based on our past experience, we disrupt the flow of life. I was certain he was wrong. In fact, the check came quickly, with no questions asked. I had to learn to look at each situation fresh.

The only time we're given by the grace of creation is now. If I practice living in awareness with an open heart, I feel a deep peace within and allow awakened presence to permeate my interactions with others. Channa has taught me tools to dwell within, where wholeness and self-worth are alive.

In that sense, I didn't *get anything* from my time with Channa. To the contrary, I left behind some of the things that were never mine in the first place. I'm able now to accept more of myself. Before encountering Channa, I felt unsettled, searching outside for a teacher, a new type of yoga, a friend, a partner, a lover. Now I feel a profound sense of wholeness, not some glossed-over well-being where life has no problems. I allow and encourage all aspects of myself to be known, the bitter and the sweet.

Just as a wave doesn't need to go looking for water, we don't need to look for anything outside ourselves. We can enjoy life's treasures as they are and as we are, right here, right now. And just as the wave rests in water watching the light change amid the movement, we too can dwell open to compassion, concentration, and awareness. It's not time that heals, it's awareness of the little things that life presents, however long each one takes. The warp and weft of the tapestry of life includes all things.

Thanks to daily practice, I now feel more connected within and able to stay present as I live my life with grace and attention. When two or three days go by without being mindful of my inner body's quality and nature, my tank feels empty. Just as we need to drink water all day long, we need to practice awareness in an ongoing manner to function fully. When spirit and compassion are connected, we're satiated. Any time is the right moment to practice awareness, otherwise the time slips away. When the mind has too many days, weeks, or months to create and embellish stories, we lose touch with the energy of our heart. The proof is in the practice. When we fail to attend to awareness, feeling unsettled is the outcome. Mammiee would always encourage me to practice what I loved the most. She lived by this—practice, practice, practice—always at her piano.

The Drip of the Teachings

At another café breakfast, a student asked Channa why she was having fewer realizations in nature than while practicing yoga and meditation, listening to his talks and attending *satsang.*[*] Channa replied that growth happens when the "drip of the teachings" is there. It's like being in a hospital, he said, when the depleted body receives electrolytes intravenously. Teachings and practice are nutrients for the body, mind, and heart.

The mind can't have a makeover or a do-over, but it can witness itself more consistently. Doing so is easier when we focus on the intelligence of the sensate body. I'm able to find meaningful responses to my inquiries when I look for "answers" in my body. The body must be included in spiritual practice.

One day in class, Channa suggested not forcing the body to open or take any particular yoga posture. We're like flowers, he

---

[*] At the café, Channa never gave a "talk." It was always a conversation with questions and responses. At *satsang*, he usually began with a talk, followed by a question-and-answer period. Even then, the talk always arose from a context, something that had come up during a yoga session or our lives together at the center.

said. If you force a flower to open by pulling on its pedals, the flower will disappear. When the flower follows the flow of its natural process, beauty arises without intervention or even effort. We're the same. Our soul opens of its own accord, and one way we can be aware of it is through mindfulness of the body.

Awareness helps us understand that we don't need to entertain anyone else's dysfunction. Through the practice, I can now witness my outer and inner worlds without *reacting*, and instead, I can simply *respond*. I've cultivated the ability to observe areas of my life in which there are inner battles and offer them space and presence. Peace, forgiveness, and compassion are living, breathing parts of the healing journey. Emotional cycles are messengers, or teachers. We'll be in cycles of healing our whole lifetimes. Like a soft pillow to lay my head on, living in awareness is a deep comfort, even when I'm witnessing something difficult.

We all have egos, feel envy, and can be abrasive, anxious, and controlling at times. What I appreciate most about Channa is not just that his approach is grounded, but that he himself is so very human on his own path, with his own pain, flaws, and conditioning. The transparency I see in him helps me feel safe, knowing that he too is a work in progress. But I didn't always see this. Sometimes I would flip-flop and see him as other worldly, almost god-like, like he could do nothing wrong, and that he was more than just human. Today as I look back on this time I think that it could have been my own introduction into nondualism, where I would have several related thoughts yet the strands would be different. Whatever I was beginning to realize, what I did know for sure is that Channa would open his heart and door to everyone, holding space to nurture a home, a community, and beyond. He is held by the universe to teach, a testament to the refuge he has created in Melbourne.

Love Is Love

During my first retreat with Channa, he gave a two-hour yoga session that weaved in teachings on envy. Afterward, we went straight from the temple room to breakfast. Channa didn't always eat with us; he'd often eat in his room with Darren. But that day he came to the dining area and when we sat down with our food, he asked what I thought about the class. I said it was great, that envy's a huge subject. Then he asked if I felt envious of anyone, and I said no, I didn't. He suggested I look more deeply, like I had missed the point. Suddenly I could see many objects of envy in my consciousness, along with my efforts to deny and suppress them, and I began crying. Later I realized that being spiritual doesn't mean to be without envy, but rather, to live a life where truth, no matter what it is, is valued.

Channa doesn't teach us to get rid of dark emotions, but through meditation and concentration, to observe the mind as it is and experience what it means to be a spirit living in a human body. With practice, I'm able to drop more often into the space of the heart, and any decisions I make come from seeing and feeling who is really inside. Mindfulness of breathing helps me connect with my beingness. As I feel the ebb and flow of breath, I touch the spirit within.

The world needs wisdom teachings now more than ever. Teachers past and present are needed to light the way to all our realizations. Channa says he isn't a guru. He doesn't want people to follow him, but to walk their own paths of consciousness. I see him as a conduit to the divine, a receiver and transmitter of light-filled teachings and messages. I don't think he chose to be what he is; I believe it chose him. The practice of living in awareness is about universal truths. We're given the space to look within and see which areas of our life divert our attention from real problems. Then we can give greater attention to what matters. It's time for us to honor who we are, take a deep breath, and begin the journey of coming home to ourselves—not to our roles or other ways we isolate ourselves with labels, but the *being* who was there long before categories arose and will be there long after.

One time at the café, Channa, Darren, and I were drinking our lattés. Channa and Darren had only been together for a few years, but because of their deep affection and trust for each other, it seemed much longer to me. After a long silence, Channa said to me, "I'm not always with partners who are gay." This was so out of the blue and I was taken aback. He continued, "Love is just love, and it's not limited to romantic love. As spirits in human form, we're symphonies of love, the living, breathing essence of love. We can always take refuge in love."

He didn't say much after that, and I pondered his words while driving home. When I picked up the kids I remember saying to them, "Love is love, love is love, love is love." It was like a mantra that took over me. I think the kids thought I had gone mad, the Australian term for crazy! I remember Leela saying "That's great Mom, but can we talk about something else now?" I remember laughing so hard when she said that, and with a twinkle in my eye and a smirk on my face, I replied, "Yes, of course we can." I also knew that this energy would be with me throughout cooking dinner and it felt so incredible to be completely filled up with love and to be sharing it with them.

We human beings can love each other for our soul connections alone; there's no need to focus on labels. Maybe the costumes we call our physical bodies can stop being judged or labelled at all. Defining ourselves and each other by our beingness makes things a lot less complicated, and the love that is deep inside can replace the prejudices inherent in categories. As I write this, I understand that my LGBTQ friends, my friends with disabilities, and my black and brown-bodied friends are indeed long overdue for "mattering" in a white, cisgendered, able-bodied world that has brought about more pain that most of us could ever fathom. Living with more awareness requires us to integrate our bodies, to learn about our prejudices, and to see what hasn't been working for the good of all humanity. Perhaps when we finally do this on an individual level one day, we'll see that just as the soul doesn't have a gender, we too might be ultimately free of labels that divide and separate us.

Sometimes when I'm using the word *my*, it's a tool. From the perspective of universal spirit, *my* can be a contaminant, presupposing ownership of things that cannot be possessed—house, daughter, husband, car, vacation. We don't *own* anything, not even our thoughts. The mind is there to witness. Even if my home is fully paid for, do I really own it? And my children? They are children, not *mine*. Nor is my husband *mine*. He's a being with whom I'm grateful to spend my life, but I don't own him or his time. Seeing this way helps take away fears and expectations. We're sharing life together, but not as owners.

We enter an impermanent world in a physical body and make use of what's available. Food grows and we eat. Plants help us heal. Nature is filled with teachers, and we can learn our lessons. But the desire to acquire more than we need to live healthy, fulfilling lives drives a wedge between us and the natural world (and between us and ourselves). Our fearful, destructive ways are driven by feelings of inadequacy and are not sustainable. Laws written and enforced out of fear lead to contraction, not love or even order. Nature provides more than enough for all. We need to stop rushing and instead enjoy nature along the way, opening ourselves to the magic of the unknown. If we live freely with the flow of life's offerings, it will change everything. When I'm flowing with what is arising, gratitude is present and an inner smile radiates. There is wholeness, ease, spaciousness, and peace. This sun doesn't discriminate over whom it will warm. This kind of love is for all.

How can we stop being defined by our struggles and other problems the mind creates? How can we be true to our nature in both easy and challenging circumstances? Even fear is just a thought. President Franklin Delano Roosevelt said, "We have nothing to fear, but fear itself." Spiritual practice helps us notice our insecurities and teaches us to hold them lovingly. I used to wish they'd go away, robbing myself of their purpose and message. Even immersed in healing modalities, I didn't feel the acceptance I feel today, thanks to living in awareness.

CHAPTER SIX

Channa Dassanayaka

After meeting Channa, the gates of spirit opened in my heart and profoundly changed the way I live. Conscious compassion and self-love have become a way of being. I didn't know this was possible. I also realized the importance beauty has for me. Now, as a ritual, I cut flowers from my garden or buy them at a store and take the time to honor the home that shelters me and the soul that animates my body. And when a flower arrangement gets old, I make another using some flowers from the old one and some new ones.

One chilly day in Melbourne, I was in the kitchen with Channa after class and he asked me to collect the old flowers from the shrine and around the house. He didn't say much, so I mimicked what I saw him doing, removing the older-looking flowers, cutting the stems of ones that had life left in them, and placing them back in the vase with fresh water. Being there, doing that, gave me a sense of calm. This was a place where I could take refuge from the world when I felt disturbed, a place where art, flowers, sculptures, and the teachings all came together like a symphony. Now at home, I feel similarly uplifted by flower arranging and even by housework. It's a small but meaningful way I take care of myself.

As you enter Channa's home, the first thing you see is an elephant shrine dedicated to his mother. This is his home yet also a public space, and it's right around the corner from the yoga room where we practice together. Channa mentions his mother in almost every class, telling the story of an experience he had with her or sharing a comment she made to help heal a situation. The elephant, her favorite animal, represents strength and courage. Sometimes I'm bowled over by the shrine's jasmine fragrance, his mother's favorite scent. The waiting area to sign in for classes has photos of Channa's family.

One time a student asked Channa to speak about his life, and he replied, "Why are you interested in my life? I have left it. But I will tell the story as though we're reading a novel." I wasn't sure what he meant, but I think he was asking us, Why the fascination with someone else's story? What about your own life? After that, he shared the story of his life.

After the Drought

Channa Dassanakayaka was born in Sri Lanka on March 24, 1969. His parents were living on the top floor of a building in the center of Colombo. On the bottom floor were shops, including a flower shop. The shop owner's daughter was getting married that day, and Channa's parents were invited to the wedding.

It was a pleasant day, although quite hot. Channa's mother had fragrant jasmine flowers in her hair and was wearing a gorgeous white sari with intricate gold threading along with precious family heirloom jewelry as she entered the church with her husband. Guests were gathering, and the smell of flowers, incense, and candles permeated the air. As soon as they were seated, the church bells began to ring as the bridal procession entered the church. At that very moment, following large periods of drought over a ten-year period, thunder clapped, and lightning struck the church, and a fire broke out as a downpour arrived, the first

storm in a decade. At that moment with church bells ringing and
the fire brigade rushing in, Channa's mother's water burst. His
father lifted her into his arms to drive her to the hospital. The fire
brigade all knew Channa's family, and a fire engine escorted the
family car to the hospital, while the other firemen stayed to fight
the fire.

Amidst the pouring rain, the baby came quickly. His mother
didn't even have time to remove her jewelry or her beautiful sari.
As they arrived at the hospital, nurses, doctors, and orderlies were
removing her jewelry and sari and the baby was born, while Mrs.
Dassanayaka still had flowers in her hair. It looked and smelled
almost like a temple celebration with the scent of jasmine and the
sights of jewelry and the beautiful silk sari and church bells and
then rain. Channa's parents said it felt very auspicious.

Channa told us he was slow learning to walk, and yet his legs
folded easily into the lotus posture, even when he was asleep. After he began walking, when he'd sit down, his right leg would still
gravitate on top of his left knee. His family was concerned about
all this and they asked an astrologer for advice. The astrologer
told them he had been a yogi in his previous life and that he had
come into this life to help people.

Channa's mother was educated at a convent and trained in
Western etiquette. She always cooked for the family, mostly traditional Sri Lankan food, and no matter how many people
appeared at the dinner table, there was always enough. Through
her, Channa developed a sense of hospitality and generosity, and
a taste for good food. But it was at his grandmother's house, eating her *soul food* and spending time in her kitchen, where Channa
found his love of cooking and his love of life. When he was a
boy, he spent weekends and holidays with his grandparents in a
village outside of Columbo. His grandfather was the village head,
like a mayor. They owned a car, a sign of wealth, and had a horse
and a couple of elephants too. His grandparents were generous
and gave land, provisions, and money to local charities, including
Buddhist temples. They employed most of the village's people in
their rice paddies, kitchen, and their many businesses, including
gem mines and tea plantations.

When the local women wanted to get a message to the village head, whether about family matters, financial problems, or civic issues, they approached Channa's grandmother, and because of her, the village ran smoothly. She was the custodian of tradition, knowing which dish to serve for each occasion and festival. When Channa's grandfather was unable to fulfill various duties, his grandmother would cover for him, attending gatherings on his behalf.

Their house was a meeting place for the community, which meant the kitchen was a hive of activity, often overflowing with people and food. Extra provisions were always on hand for family members and others who might drop by. Every week, his grandparents offered a meal for the whole village.

Channa's grandma had a huge set of keys, which she kept in her sari. The longest one, for the front door of their compound, was held in a front fold, and the remaining fifteen or twenty keys hung around her tiny waist. Those keys opened the rooms and the cupboards, where she kept everything from rice and gems to precious family memories.

Of his grandparents' nine children, thirty-one grandchildren, and thirty-six great-grandchildren, Channa was among his grandma's favorites. She never had to yell at him, as she did the other children, who were always diving into the nearby river and getting into trouble. Channa's grandmother taught him cultural protocols and the ingredients and significance of Sri Lankan village cuisine. She was always a source of inspiration through her wisdom, passion, and enthusiasm. Keenly interested in learning to cook, Channa listened attentively as she shared recipes and preparation techniques with the women and men who worked in her kitchen. From his tiny kitchen at the yoga center in Melbourne, he cooked for about thirty-five students each Sunday. Alongside his profound gift of teaching about mind, body, and spirit, his other creative expression is cooking. For a period of time when he first left Sri Lanka, he was a chef and restauranteur in both Melbourne and Europe.

Solace

Channa's early years were steeped in Sinhalese Buddhist traditions. His grandmother nurtured his soul by her presence, always pointing out to him life's truths through simple daily tasks. And his parents taught him about prayer and service. Each full moon day, when workers in Sri Lanka stay at home with their families to pray in the Buddhist way, Channa and his brothers had to make their own beds, taking on duties their servants normally performed. Channa still cleans his house as a daily ritual.

From 1983-2009, Sri Lanka was torn apart by a brutal civil war. In 1994, his father was shot, then died of a heart attack two years later. So, in 1996 with the encouragement of his mother amidst the country's instability, Channa packed his bags and moved to Australia. He was twenty-seven. Then, the following year his mother died in a tragic car accident, and Channa returned to Sri Lanka to heal from these losses.

One of his first stops was the monastery outside his grandma's village. He needed a place of solace for inner exploration, and he thought about spending time there to meditate on life's questions and find peace in his grief. After living in Australia, he came back to Sri Lanka wearing jewelry, a wristwatch, and sunglasses, and the abbot, a senior monk who was over 100 years old, told him that he looked as though he were dressed for a cocktail party. The abbot had only one tooth and Channa wasn't absolutely sure what he said, but he did hear the words "slow down" and "meditate."

Channa realized that until that moment he'd been living for his parents, and it wasn't serving him. Now that his parents had passed away, he wanted to reexamine everything. All that he'd been told—do this, have that, be somebody—hadn't prepared him for the grief he was feeling. So he asked the abbot if he could ordain as a monk and stay at the monastery for a few months. The abbot declined his request to join the monastic order, but accepted Channa as an *upasaka*, wearing the white robes of a lay adherent and following ten moral precepts:

Refraining from:
1. harming living things
2. taking what is not given
3. sexual misconduct
4. lying or gossip
5. taking intoxicating substances
6. taking substantial food after midday
7. dancing, singing, and music
8. use of garlands, perfumes, and personal adornment
9. use of luxurious beds and seats
10. accepting and holding money, gold, or silver

And he allowed him to stay at the monastery to meditate and try to find peace and meaning to his life.

His grandmother, who was the monastery's prime benefactor, telegrammed the abbot, saying she'd just lost her daughter, Channa's mother, and didn't want to lose her grandson too. "Therefore, if you don't send him back to me, I will stop all alms offerings to the monks." The abbot summoned Channa and said, "You have a lot of obstacles, and one is your grandmother. Teaching you is my duty. Dealing with her request is yours. How can we help each other?" Channa asked the abbot to ignore his grandmother, but he said he couldn't. "I need to eat, my monks need to eat, and if she withdraws her offerings, I won't be able to feed them. You're bringing us a lot of problems."

Spiritual Gifts

Despite those problems, the abbot recognized Channa's spiritual gifts, and allowed him to stay. When villagers would come to the monastery and ask for blessings, the abbot would send them to "that boy in the corner with the white robes, because he has blessings to give." Channa would invite the villagers to sit with him, and he offered flowers and incense to the shrine. His reputation began to grow; people found it calming to be in his presence.

One day the abbot asked him, "Do you hear that sound? It's not a bird," and Channa replied, "Yes." The elder monk asked, "Do you think it's a frog?" and Channa said, "I think nothing, I'm just experiencing its raw form." The abbot then said to Channa, "Do you see your thoughts going through your mind?" "Yes," he said, and the abbot asked, "Do you know what they are?"

"They're just floating," Channa said. The abbot replied, "Do you want to take one and identify with it?" Channa told him, "If you want me to, I will. But there's no reason to."

"Do you hear the dog barking in the distance?" the abbot then asked. Channa replied, "I hear a sound, but I don't want to say it's barking or it's not."

The abbot gathered the other monks and said, "This boy has entered the stream." Channa thought the abbot wanted him to bow to the other monks, but the abbot asked the monks to bow to him. Then he asked Channa, "Do you feel like you 'got it'?" and Channa replied, "No, but I'm getting it." The abbot agreed. "If you'd said you 'got it,' I would have said no."

Channa became very clear in his meditation, and learned from the abbot's way of working with him. He always knew what the elder monk was going to ask him. By now, his grandmother had begun withholding provisions from the temple. Soon she came to visit, and Channa went to bow at her feet out of respect. The abbot said no, and asked his grandmother to prostrate before him. Channa's grandmother was perplexed by this turn of events, but the abbot said that her grandson had attained the stage of the Buddha's path called stream-entry and it would be inappropriate for him to bow to her. Channa's grandmother bowed. The abbot was respected throughout the village, and his temple was the one Channa's grandmother had grown up nearby. In her heart, she knew Channa was able to understand profound spiritual truths.

Even though this monastery and many other temples in the area were supported by Channa's grandparents, Channa never received special treatment. By then he had diabetes, and the villagers' offerings, high in carbohydrates and other sugars, were taking their toll on his health. As the most junior practitioner, he was the last person to be served food, and often he didn't get enough. He had hoped he might get three meals a day instead of the single midday meal of a monk, due to his condition, but that wasn't allowed, and with this challenge he experienced a sense of surrender. He felt no desire or remorse, and for the first time he felt truly alive.

Channa's sleeping quarters were next to the kitchen, which was busy and noisy. He lacked seniority, but did have his own room, although it was just a slab with an attached toilet. In the middle of the night, an onslaught of insects and creatures would visit. Like all the temple residents, he had a cup to catch them rather than kill them, and throughout the night he would empty his cup outside. As a child of privilege, he'd always been to some extent in control of his life. But with the loss of his parents and the rigors of monastic life, he woke up inside.

Eventually, Channa left the monastery so his grandmother would resume providing food for the monks. And the abbot agreed that Channa had unfinished business in Australia and needed to get back. With the support and encouragement of a friend, he opened Dassanayaka Yoga Centre in Melbourne, which to my mind is his true calling. At the center, he not only serves as spiritual guide, he takes every opportunity to cook for his students and friends.

CHAPTER SEVEN

Witnessing

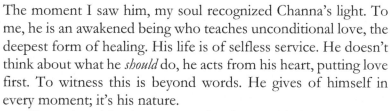

The moment I saw him, my soul recognized Channa's light. To me, he is an awakened being who teaches unconditional love, the deepest form of healing. His life is of selfless service. He doesn't think about what he *should* do, he acts from his heart, putting love first. To witness this is beyond words. He gives of himself in every moment; it's his nature.

Channa's spiritual awareness has been with him his whole life. When Channa was a boy, saints blessed him and assured his parents he was spiritually gifted and would help heal people. His mother and grandmother nurtured him on all levels, and today he embodies their depth and energy in all he touches. When he offers a healing in class, many of us avert our eyes as there is so much energy radiating from his being. His presence is so impressive people bow at his feet in gratitude, though he seems uncomfortable when they do.

Humility

On my second retreat with Channa, he gave me the responsibility of smudging the room with incense, offering fresh fruit and flowers at the shrine, sweeping the floor, and making his tea—English breakfast with milk or the wonderful ginger lemongrass and lime tea the Balinese would make for him and all of us. Channa loves sipping tea while teaching, although today his diet has changed and he doesn't have milk with his tea. Another job I had was placing red paste I'd mixed with water on the students' third eye (middle of the forehead) as a *puja* blessing. I would chant *Om Shanti Om*—Peace for All Beings—silently while doing so.

Suddenly, out of nowhere, many students were bowing to their knees and touching Channa's feet. Some of the more seasoned students did this first, quite naturally, seeing the teacher as a reflection of their higher self. When this is done we are bowing not to the personality of the teacher, we are bowing to the spiritual understanding that is held in his heart that we hope might transfer to us. Also in showing reverence for our teacher, it isn't to inflate his ego, but rather for the students to feel into their humility. So on this particular day the beginning students seemed to be following the leader, not their own realization. Channa is extremely humble and realized the newer students were not bowing out of their own truth. He got up from his seat and asked me if I would whisper to each student to please stop. So I did. Placing my hands in prayer position and bowing my head sightly, I asked them to stop.

Later that retreat, when we'd all returned to the temple room after the afternoon break, getting ready for meditation, I forgot to make Channa's milk-tea. A new student had just arrived and was going to film for the center's website, and while I was assisting him I forgot to pass the task onto someone else. As soon as the meditation was over, Channa said, "Who forgot my tea?" I was mortified. I raised my hand and tried to accept the reminder humbly.

To me, the teaching wasn't about having things "just so" or needing to be perfect, but remembering to stay open and live in awareness. Channa smiled, and the other students laughed anxiously. Through the rest of the retreat, each time I walked in with his tea, I was greeted with smiles of joy (or perhaps relief). It was a genuinely pleasant exchange.

Channa made the choice to leave the monastery. Staying there, besides his grandmother's withholding of alms, would not have been true to his life's purpose. His wisdom, compassion, and kindness embody grace and the sacred truth of the teachings. His classes are relevant for modern life, and at the same time supported by his guides. He lives in the moment, and even the finances of the center reflect what he teaches. He would give his last dollar to someone in need, and he has. Royalties from his book, *Sri Lankan Flavours: A Journey Through the Island's Food and Culture,* went to the people along the damaged coastlines after the 2010 tsunami. He traveled there and set up kitchens and food stations to give people hot meals through the devastation, until some kind of normal life was restored.

Channa lived in a tiny shack at the back of the Dassanayaka Yoga Centre property. It was his healing oasis, and after a day of teaching and giving, he went there to rest deeply, enjoying his own retreat, in a manner of speaking, from the responsibilities of the yoga center. Inside the shack, it was quite modern—with a couch, bed, air conditioning, and heating. The floor was covered by carpets and yoga mats and was kind of bouncy.

His mother told him, "If you have work to do, do it from your bed. If that isn't possible, walk to another room in your home and do it there. The further you have to go from bed to work, the more problems arise." He took her advice to heart, and every day he went from the meditation and yoga room to his bed, and from his bed to the meditation and yoga room. He said it felt balancing to do this, and the classes he taught didn't consume him.

Channa practices what he teaches. He made a vow to be of service to all beings, not just the students attending his classes. He lives the practice all day, not just in the hours he's teaching. I witnessed his days filled with classes, healings, cooking, and rituals.

The oil lamp in the meditation room burned 24/7 in honor of his teachers. Every morning upon rising, Channa lights candles for each of his teachers. Photos of saints, Jesus, Buddha, Mother Mary, his own mother, Sivakami Sonia Sumar, and figurines of Hindu deities are on display for all to appreciate with deep respect. Although Channa was raised in the Buddhist tradition, he doesn't offer only Buddhism. He teaches how to live in awareness daily.

The garden at the Dassanayaka Yoga Centre is abundant with fruits, vegetables, and spices, as well as lotus flowers. Watching Channa care for his home and garden taught me a lot. I used to despise cleaning, not realizing that attention to detail can be a sacred act. No matter how many classes Channa teaches or how many healings he gives or meals he prepares, he always makes time to care for the home and garden that hold him. Channa recognizes that everything in the world has an energy, and our home space needs our kind attention as much as our inner sanctum.

Watching my teacher perform these simple acts helped bring devotion into my own daily chores. Now in my daily rituals—making the bed, hugging and loving our children, making coffee for Mike, walking the dog, cleaning the kitchen, and vacuuming—I connect deeply with myself and all of existence. As I dust surfaces, wash dishes, and fold laundry, I treat each as an act of prayer, and I joyfully awaken to the moment. I used to play loud music and watch the clock, waiting for the chores to be over. Treating them as rituals reminds me how much I value the connection with my higher self and the space in which I dwell.

Trust

Not long after becoming Channa's student, I came to realize the importance of exploring what's going on *inside*—blockages, physical and emotional pain, energy needing release, mind chatter—allowing each layer of patterning and conditioning to reveal itself. Living in awareness is not about amassing information but experiencing the *body in the body** in the present moment. Witnessing

---

* Expression used by the Buddha in the *Scripture on the Full Awareness of Breathing (Sattipatthana Sutta)*

my own inner space, I can feel my body, heart, mind, emotions, and environment, and taste the nectar of my being. As my relation to the present moment deepens, trust builds within.

Just two weeks after we met, Channa gave me the key to his home and center. When I told a friend in America, she said, "He already trusts you." I thought about her response. Channa's friends, teachers, and monks all had keys too; I wasn't the only one. Yet I knew he had given me more than a key to the center. He had entrusted me with the key to his heart, and mine. I felt reborn; some of my negative conditioning fell away. Trust issues were beginning to heal, and my faith in the path of awakening rose exponentially. I felt a higher love had guided me to Channa, and because of his trust, I felt safer in the world.

Until then, I'd been afraid to trust myself or others. The small act of giving me a housekey helped me breathe and begin trusting the good in myself and others. It was a *coming home inside* and allowed me to get closer to the blueprint of who I am and see some things I thought were me, but weren't. I learned that opening to truth and innocence is our birthright.

Now it takes me just one conscious breath to remember that everything is okay. When I practice living in awareness, even when I'm in the midst of "not knowing," I allow space rather than push these challenging experiences away. *Not knowing* takes the pressure off needing to know everything. We can take risks, try new things, and be more open and alive in each moment. Even when habitual thoughts and patterns arise, I'm able to witness without giving them inordinate weight. There's more to each moment than our thoughts.

A student asked Channa, "When is life going to feel easier for me?" Channa said the idea of things getting easier is an illusion. The more aware we become, the more we're able to learn from whatever arises. He advised him to stop creating stories out of hard times and instead to get on with life itself, to accept things as they are and not what the mind thinks they ought to be. An immense love dwells within each of us, but we get in our own way. Awakening is possible when we don't need things to be easier, or perfect. Then we can appreciate the perfection of what's there and co-create the space for healing. With this way of being in the world, answers to our questions present themselves.

The student continued, "Sometimes I feel trapped by my own pain." Channa suggested he practice *witnessing*. "Witnessing is not ignoring your pain, trying to make it pleasant, or wishing it away. It's validating your pain without being bound by it."

What we seek is already inside us and presents itself in our grounded body. Channa, too, needs to witness himself and recognize anxiety or fear when they arise. With awareness, he can allow them to leave his body gently, without blindly believing the stories they tell. Witnessing emotions is the first step in creating space around them. If they don't take hold of us, we can dwell in this deep pool of awareness, allowing each moment to be exactly as it is.

Every day the practice shows me new ways to work with challenges. It softens my heart's memory of deep pains and cultivates space rather than suppressing feelings. Witnessing rather than reacting, I can assess how to respond to stimuli, and whether a thought or a strong feeling is carrying a message or is just a habituated response based on something that happened long ago.

We were born with this kind of freedom, but through conditioning we've forgotten. When we simply *witness* the moment and all that it holds, living in awareness, without blaming or judging, our humanness returns. When I forget to witness, my days are difficult. I perceive certain thoughts and feelings as enemies. Living in awareness, I see what's bothering me; then I can look at it while being kind to myself. Without struggling, I mindfully respect each moment as a gift from consciousness. When I'm truthful, I see that nothing is against me. All demands for how the moment *should* be have a message beneath them. Every thought, symptom, and individual offers a divine and practical teaching.

Be a Friend

When we first moved to Melbourne, Charlie was finding it hard to adjust to a new school, a new home, and a new country. I was reacting less compassionately than I might have, wishing he would just get on board with it all. I spoke with Channa about it, and he told me, "He wants a friend, Mellara. Can you be his friend?" So simple.

When I picked up the children from school that afternoon, I stopped trying to fill some big parenting role, and realized that love is all that's real. That's what my son needed, and that's what I gave him, and I fell to my knees in gratitude for Channa's advice. The experience made me wonder whether all the most difficult situations in life can be mended with love. Charlie and I enjoyed being around each other again, and his hard times were soon a memory.

After practicing living in awareness for a year, I was able to apply it to nearly every situation. When I was about to react, I'd pause, take a mindful breath, and practice witnessing. I wasn't running away, just taking stock. I used to act quickly on my impulses, and not necessarily compassionately, even with those who mean so much to me. Sometimes it was out of habit. My conditioned beliefs brought pain from situations that, when I looked deeply, I saw weren't even related.

In the beginning, I felt a lot of unease in my body, perhaps because I didn't accept myself really. At times in meditation, I saw myself trying to control or fix things and realized I'm no longer the six-year-old girl at the mercy of my mum. Nor am I my wounded great-grandfather from Denmark, trying to migrate to Australia. It took dedication and practice, and then something started shifting inside. With unwavering focus, I stayed on the path, trusting Channa and his teachings. Uniting Awareness is not just what Channa teaches, it is also the name of the healing wellness center located in Melbourne dedicated to uniting the awareness of all beings. They offer yoga and meditation classes, retreats, workshops and private healing sessions with Channa.

Embrace It All

Another time at the café, Channa told a group of us that if we have any doubts about ourselves, anything we aren't willing to own as our truth, we split ourselves inside. Compartmentalization turns us against the flow of life, and we suffer. We can feel it at the core of our being, building up pressure in the body.

Before encountering Channa's teachings, I would divide myself into compartments, like the social media persona, the persona I wore around family and friends, and at work and even with myself. Now when I notice, I also feel the unconditional love inside that nurtures and accepts all of me. I no longer fight to protect parts of myself from dangers that are no longer there. As the pain and unease I felt before beginning the practice slowly disappear and I accept the parts of myself I've been rejecting, embracing the wholeness of my being, loving the unlovable, I experience miracles. Channa teaches that a true miracle is not one we need to perform, but something to *be*, to notice. "Don't try to find miracles outside yourself," he says. "Just walk, live, and breathe the way you are, and as possible, do it consciously."

I have begun to heal from within and at the same time, mend my broken family of origin and some of the friendships that have been torn apart. Now I can go out in the world enjoying a path that does not exclude anything. I'm no longer cutting people out of my heart, as I used to do a lot. Our hearts can hold it all, so much more than we might ever imagine.

The Flavor of Love

Channa adapts his teaching to situations, people, cultures, and places. Once he told me he only diets when he's asleep. He loves cooking and sharing Sri Lankan cuisine. It's a way for him to use food as medicine, going in deep where the teachings cannot. After his stay in an Ayurvedic hospital in Bali in 2017, he realized that his body stays healthier on a vegetarian diet, and he hasn't craved meat since. As a result, he was able to have his insulin pump removed.

During my first eight months in Melbourne, we went to the Red Door Café after yoga classes. After that, we started going to the Thompson Street Café, which is a ten-minute drive from the studio, a small restaurant infused with Melbourne's creativity and acceptance, as well as nutritious, delicious food. The first time I came along to the Thompson Street Café, I was introduced to everyone there, and I could see how special Channa was to them and how connected they felt to him. No one there knew Channa as a spiritual teacher, but he has a way about him, a lightness, that everyone feels attracted to, like an old friend. When Channa was sick, their nourishing fare helped nurse him back to health. As a thank-you, Channa prepared a dinner for the restaurant's staff at his home, and invited Mike and me to join them.

When Channa cooks, the flavors and recipes are magnificent, a spiritual surrender with each bite—the love, care, and beauty that is the life he creates in every moment. It was Friday rush hour, and Mike and I sat in traffic for two hours. Mike was pretty grumpy when we finally arrived. The moment we walked in, Channa greeted us and offered Mike a beer. It was such a huge relief for Mike, being offered a beer by a spiritual teacher. With that small gesture, Mike felt included, accepted for who he was. This wasn't Mike's first meeting with Channa, but it was his first informal gathering. Mike had attended a day-long weekend re-treat with Channa a few months after I met my teacher. Because of Mike's long work hours and full-time job, he never attended classes during the week, and on weekends it was family time where we did things like go to the beach with Charlie and Leela, drove through Victoria's bushlands, and visited the many food markets that Melbourne is famous for.

Channa cares deeply for every living being; I've never seen him impose his belief system on anyone. It was amazing to be around these people—the restaurant owner, the young chef, the kitchen and wait staff, a mix of meditation, yoga, and non-yoga people, human beings from all walks of life coming together to celebrate life in an atmosphere of acceptance and love. Channa helps create space where everyone can be who they are. There was a genuine sense that night that we all belonged. In his simple yet profound way, Channa brings people from all walks of life together.

CHAPTER EIGHT
A New Center

Channa doesn't own much, but he often says to me, "The earth is here for us to live like kings and queens, while *never* taking it for granted." His mother always told him, "If you sit with your spine upright, with grace, you're sovereign of your own kingdom wherever you are."

Around Channa, I feel his spiritual riches, as though I'm in the presence of greatness. There's a wondrous bounty in everything he touches. When he exits a room, he leaves it with more energy and beauty than before he entered. I've witnessed him transmute fear and tension into kindness, gentleness, patience, and love, even while confronting uncomfortable issues. And at the same time, he's very humble.

Texture of Silence

During my time in Melbourne, I loved sipping tea with my teacher in the backyard of the center, among the lotus flowers. Being surrounded by life's blessings and abundance was grounding for me. What I love most about Channa's teachings is that everything is valued equally; nothing is bigger than the smallest details of life or separate from anything else. This is the harmony of life engendered by being one with all existence.

We often sat in silence. At first I found it uncomfortable; it was a muscle I hadn't used much. The silence felt like nothing was happening, like one of us needed to speak, and it brought out my insecurity. But over time, a feeling of intimacy was established, not romantic intimacy but the love of love itself, love inside its own energy. I realized that I often talk my way out of being in the moment, and that talking can be an escape from beingness. Sipping tea or entering any moment can be a meditation. It doesn't need to be separate from everyday life activities. In experiencing these wordless moments, my senses heightened—smelling the garden, tasting the tea, hearing the birdsong, and feeling the ground beneath my bare feet.

In this silence, Channa appeared to be giving me nothing, but in the presence of nothingness everything was present. Even though I enjoy talking, in those moments,words, even said with kindness, would have distanced us from the moment. *Feeling* the experience was enough, and within the silence I felt space around my heart. There was no fear or insecurity, just the rhythms of life and the currents of energy, juxtaposed with the overstimulation of so many other life situations.

When we first started sitting together in silence, I didn't understand its importance, and I would get impatient. Now I realize Channa was helping me learn to be more settled within. After a while, I became mesmerized by each moment, savoring the beauty of it all without looking for anything else to do. Learning to feel the texture of silence was profound for me, and I can now be present with this at any time, whether people are around or not. I can connect with the healing qualities of nature. I have heard Channa say that to heal the world, we need to feel the joy we came into the world with.

High Tea

In November 2015, twenty-three students plus Channa were ready to depart from Melbourne and from cities around the world to attend the Dassanayaka Yoga Centre's semiannual retreat in Bali, when Mt. Agung, an active volcano in Bali, began erupting and all flights into Bali were cancelled. The retreat center had already bought all the fruit, vegetables, and flowers for us, prepared our rooms, and brought in a massage therapist to aid in our healing. To help them recoup their costs, we agreed to pay the center 40 percent of these total expenses. Some of us had purchased travel insurance, and when we received our claim money, many gave it to Channa to donate to the center in Bali, but there was still a shortfall. So the Dassanayaka Yoga community in Melbourne organized a benefit High Tea.

The afternoon of the tea was sunny. People came and enjoyed this unusual offering, and we raised 6,000 Australian dollars auctioning donated items and services.*

Channa put me in charge of his beloved grandmother's precious tea sets. My job was to clean the cups, saucers, and pots, and place them on the tables. I was trying to be extra careful, afraid something might break, and my fear was realized! Be careful what's on your mind. Even with all the meditation I'd been doing, I witnessed fear arise, and I took the bait like a fish plunging toward a hook. I picked up two saucers, unaware they'd stuck together, and one suddenly fell onto the other with a huge crash. It played out in front of me as though in slow motion, and there was nothing I could do about it. I was horrified. I'd wanted to do my job perfectly and lost touch with the only thing that's real, which is unconditional love.

Channa walked by and told me it was okay. He said that breaking the saucer allowed him to become less attached to things, even a gift from his grandmother. It didn't help; I continued to beat myself up. As the day went on, I was able to observe that my feelings of guilt were not based on anything in the moment but were conjured in my mind. The actual circumstances didn't bring about guilt or shame, my thoughts did, and I was able to feel the distinction.

---

*See the YouTube video to promote the tea, at
https://www.youtube.com/watch?v=jfwQPItiKYY&feature=youtu.be

Then I remembered Channa's teaching that guilt is a trick of the mind, and I tried to see how I might let it go. The deepest cause of my feeling guilty, I ascertained, was not loving myself unconditionally, which meant I had to be perfect in the eyes of others to feel okay about myself. But this "perfection" is not *who I am*. Feeling shame inside doesn't allow love in. How could an accident like breaking a saucer give rise to such deep emotions?

That day, I was exonerated from my sentence of guilty as charged. I saw that the only judicial sentencing was within myself. When thoughts bombard us, they are only thoughts, and witnessing them allows us to see that they're not actually in the moment. They're feelings from the past, and that day I determined that when guilt arises, I will surround it with awareness and transform it into its opposite, which is love. I wondered whether this was why I'd always been an overachiever, trying to prove that I'm more than I already am.

Petals of Many Colors

At another breakfast gathering, Channa told a student that we're not here to conquer life but to be defeated by it. When we embark on a spiritual journey, in most cases, we've gone through something and hit rock bottom. Shedding the ego and looking within help us figure out who we really are. We do not conquer life in the way that we thought we were supposed to, but having been "defeated," we can now live our soul's journey fully.

Being with Channa and the community, I was learning so many things I hadn't heard elsewhere. I had never allowed myself to *enjoy* the creative journey of my life before. Whatever I experienced, I compared it with self-created goals, came up short, anxiety arose, and I felt miserable. I was my own worst enemy, making life impossible, continuously *seeking* without allowing the path to just unfold.

About ten months into living in Melbourne, Mike and I were excited to host Thanksgiving with our new Aussie friends that we made. Mike is an incredible cook especially if he has the time to do it. I think as an American kid growing up he was deeply influenced by the way his mother loved all things Thanksgiving. I would have loved to have met her and Mike's dad, but they had passed away a few years before Mike and I met. It was her favorite holiday and I think she passed the tradition down to her children and especially Mike.

Our Thanksgiving dinner in Australia came about in a natural way, starting when my yoga friend Barbara mentioned to me that she had never tasted pumpkin pie. Australians eat pumpkin in a more savory kind of way, so she was kind of perplexed when I mentioned to her that pumpkin pie was sweet and often served with whipped cream and or vanilla ice cream. She seemed stunned, and we laughed out loud. With much excitement I said, "We must have you, Simon, and the kids over for a traditional Thanksgiving dinner with all the trimmings!" She accepted, and we invited her husband and two kids as well as Anna, her bestie, and Cathy, another friend from the yoga center, along with her partner.

It was such a wonderful experience and I felt so proud of Mike for cooking for everyone. I remember that we had to special order the turkey three weeks before because turkey isn't so much a big deal in Australia, since Thanksgiving is essentially an American holiday. On Thanksgiving Day I assisted Mike in making the sweet potato casserole with marshmallows, mashed potatoes, gravy from the drippings of the turkey, and of course the famous homemade pumpkin pies. To prepare for the big day we also made a stop to U.S.A Foods, a store that sells everything an American might be missing from home. You name it, they had it, like Lucky Charms cereal, Goldfish Cheddar Baked snacks for the kids, and French's Crispy Fried Onions for the green bean casserole. Let's not forget the Ocean Spray Whole Berry Cranberry Sauce and festive turkey paper goods for the table! We went all out, and the six kids in total had their own table just outside from us where Leela taught everyone to make turkey handprint puppets. I still to this day cherish our Thanksgiving with our Aussie friends and felt happy to be able to offer this beloved holiday that is dear to us and to so many Americans.

During a retreat one time, Channa placed flower petals of many colors on the floor, along with marigolds, orchids, and a variety of flowers indigenous to Bali, to form the shape of one large flower. It was so beautiful. He does things like this daily. There's a freshness about him. He exudes vitality. He says if you're going to do something, do it all the way, no halves and doubts, and then negative feelings will depart on their own. We did Thanksgiving that year all the way.

Darkness and Light

Another day at the coffee shop, I asked Channa about darkness. "There are days I wake up feeling so low and unsettled," I said, "that it's like the lights have been turned off." He told us not to be consumed by the dark, that it's an illusion. Although we may feel undone by it while going through it, it's also an opportunity to love and accept ourselves on a deeper level. In the world, if we aren't "together" or looking happy, people treat us as though something's deeply wrong and tell us we need to "get positive." But when we're in this kind of darkness, the best thing we can offer ourselves is to be our own dear friend, to be kind to ourselves. While staying present with these deep feelings, we can— figuratively or better still, literally—light a candle, and slowly the darkness will lift. At the very least, we can sit with ourselves honestly and allow things to be as they are. "Letting go" of the darkness might be too tall an order. "Letting it be" might be more attainable. The simple act of lighting a candle can bring forth a sense of being in the light, taking care of the world by taking care of ourselves.

At the end of many classes at the yoga center, Channa reaches out to someone and engages them in conversation. One day he spoke to a student who was new to the practice, and after a while he asked the young man what he did for a living. "Nothing, at the moment," he said. "I'm unemployed." Channa told him that many of the hardest working people he knows are unemployed. "There's pressure to be productive, and looking for a job can be stressful." He encouraged the young man to focus on life's bigger lessons.

Another student told a joke. Two men meet on a street, and one asks, "How are you?" and the other says, "I'm fine, thanks." "And how's your son?" "He's still at home and unemployed, but he's found a spiritual teacher and has begun meditating regularly." "What's meditation?" the first asks. "I don't know," says his friend. "But it's better than sitting around doing nothing!" The class roared with laughter. Channa loves jokes as a way of teaching. In my mind, he's a natural comedian, and the student's joke about meditation lightened the atmosphere for the unemployed student. Buddha nature is not only serious. Joyous humor is also needed.

Every time I talk about Channa, I feel a profound healing within me, and it carries forward to others I encounter. Thinking about Channa, I feel my own confidence, compassion, and spiritual understanding grow, and for this I am grateful. I was fortunate to be invited to so many intimate conversations at the café with other students, and these were often the wisest teachings we heard from him.

To me, Channa represents the pure energy of love. I experience him as everyone's father and everyone's child. Archetypally, he stands in for my mother and my father at times, and when this is the case, he is not a real person, he's the loving parents I never had and need to see and feel so I can find these traits within. But at the end of the day, my teacher is simply human, and although I have found no one else whose spiritual teachings are so right for me, I know that he deserves the same compassion and connection that he teaches.

Channa has formed a community around him that's worldwide. It's a diverse crowd from all walks of life. While helping at the front desk of the center one day, I noticed that there are almost fifty doctors in the center's contact list ranging from Western healers to Eastern specialists. Some of Australia's finest healthcare practitioners are in his classes daily, but you'd never know it, as this practice fosters humility. Creative types also flock to his classes for inspiration. I overheard a student say she experiences most of her most creative breakthroughs during yoga practice guided by Channa.

Channa's heartfelt energy can't help but trickle down to the local surrounding shops, businesses, and community. I've heard from many neighbors that since the yoga center moved in, the area has flourished. When someone in the center becomes ill or just needs a shoulder to cry on, someone is there to hold them in a healing space. I have a feeling that Channa's choice many years ago not to wear religious garments means he can dive more deeply into the community, even to places where robes might feel less comfortable or trustworthy. It's as though he has a backstage pass with access to all areas of healing for all beings.

A gentle soul with bipolar personality disorder told me that if it hadn't been for Channa, he wouldn't be alive today. I was helping Channa in the garden one day, and this huge man wearing jeans and a t-shirt with a roaring lion on it came to visit. The t-shirt, to me, symbolized the inner courage this man must have had to turn away from the dark and follow the light-filled path. He was soft-spoken, with scruffy hair, tattoos on the parts of his body I could see, and dark lines under his eyes indicating he'd been through a lot. He was someone from the nearby community, not Channa's yoga student—he had accidently stumbled onto the studio en route home to his wife and family. Lion Man had already spent time in jail for a crime related to his fractured mental state. He was out of work; it was a constant battle for him to keep a job. He was suicidally depressed, and he described to Channa how he envisioned walking into a police station with a plastic gun so the police would shoot him.

Lion Man told me that without constant care and guidance from Channa, his little ones would have missed out on having a dad. As an offering to Channa and the center, he left a few cut flowers on the doorstep every day. I've witnessed others like Lion Man who knock on Channa's doorstep for this kind of help, or a hot meal or a chat or even a room. Channa offers these things and often a deeper healing.

Another dear soul had left home, where she felt her life was in danger. She needed nurturing on all levels, and ended up staying at the center for six months. Eventually she left, looking stronger and more trusting, went back to school, and now is training to be a social worker. People come from all over the world and all stations of life to be in Channa's presence, and his door is always open.

Part Three

Deepening

~

Have gratitude for your so-called failures. They are your best teachers, illuminating your darkness and opening you up to conscious expansion.

CHAPTER NINE

Unconditioned Space

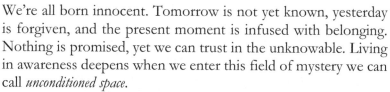

We're all born innocent. Tomorrow is not yet known, yesterday is forgiven, and the present moment is infused with belonging. Nothing is promised, yet we can trust in the unknowable. Living in awareness deepens when we enter this field of mystery we can call *unconditioned space*.

I remember dwelling in unconditioned space as a child. I'd play outside for hours never feeling criticized or judged. Being with nature's sounds and smells, the crisp air and the feeling of my bare feet on the sand or early-morning dew, I felt the love everywhere. Unfortunately, these moments were few and far between. Mostly I was in an ongoing war with my mum, my dad, and myself.

Spirit Dancing in the Pleasures of the Body

One spring day at the end of class at the yoga center, a small group of us gathered at the café with Channa. One student asked how he could stay connected to the practice while he's at home. Channa replied, "Gently, with consciousness, allow things to be as they are. Your breath is breathing, and light is coming through the window. Enjoy the songs of the birds, the colors of the flowering trees, and the multidimensional energies, vibrations, and aromas permeating the air. When you're not interfering, it's all available and you can tune in to the most beautiful experience a human being can have, dwelling in unconditioned space with no worries. Feel the sun's warmth—springtime in the cells of your body—and you'll move seamlessly into being and spirit."

When I heard this, I realized our *being* extends beyond our physical form. When we're caught up in the machinations of mind, we forget this. When I refer to *mind,* I mean "small mind," which is like a balcony in winter. We can step onto it for a while, but if we stay out too long, we freeze and lose ourselves. When I focus on sensations—spirit dancing in the pleasures of the body—I know who I am inside. Being in unconditioned space means staying in alignment with the profundity of each moment and not wanting it to be different.

The small mind usually wants things to be different from the way they are. In class one day, Channa said the mind is like a donkey (this cracked me up!), always thinking it will get the carrot. Whether or not it gets the carrot, nothing is amiss. We need to befriend the mind, recognizing it as a bridge to body and spirit.

Life is not a numbered puzzle or series of dots to connect. The universe and planets don't move in straight lines. But we walk around expecting life to go our way, whatever that means. An essential part of living in awareness is to connect inside, not through the mind, but through the heart's warmth linking us to our primordial nature.

We can do this by sitting quietly, closing our eyes, and feeling the space inside, dropping into each sense one at a time—hearing, smelling, tasting. One day as a plane flew overhead, I had a pure auditory experience without identifying it as a plane or thinking about its story. Another time, when my mind was more active, I was drawn into naming it a plane and then reliving the experience I had on my first airplane ride. Whether we are witnessing the sound or observing the activities of mind, we can bring our focus back to our breathing. As we direct consciousness inside what we are touching, seeing, smelling, tasting, or hearing, unconditioned space will present itself.

The more I dwell in unconditioned space, the more my discursive mind pauses. I feel more creative and productive, and less fatigued. It's a deeper, more restful, and sensory way of living. My mind is awake but not all over the map without cessation. We can access unconditioned space in meditation and throughout the day, with practice.

The Flow of Life

At another breakfast gathering, a student told Channa that since beginning the practice, his life wasn't like anything he'd experienced before. He added that his strengths were in learning, research, analysis, and strategic planning, and in the practice, he was appreciating quieting his mind and being more attentive, but it was difficult for him. "I like to think about things," he said. "For example, I want to know about the history of these practices. But I'm learning from your classes that practice is more about *unlearning*, not hiding behind knowledge."

Channa replied that ordinary mind functions from the past. "Life has no obligation to fit in with our conclusions," he said, "so it becomes confusing and doubts arise. We apply knowledge from areas where we have ready-made answers to areas where this information doesn't apply. Life never asks the same question twice; nothing in nature remains the same. Hence, knowledge, even from the *Bhagavad Gita*, the holy *Qur'an*, the *Bible*, or the *Vedas*, will invariably fall short. You cannot preempt a life with fixed answers. You understand things when you've lived them. That doesn't make you knowledgeable. It doesn't come from a university degree. It comes from wisdom and maturity."

Channa then asked all of us, "Can you watch the sunlight moving across the café windows without adding a story to it? Can you hear the clock ticking without saying it's a clock? Can you listen to passing cars without calling them traffic? Can you observe your breath and see your memories like a photo album, without commenting on the photos? Can you allow thoughts to enter and pass, and be open to the moment?

"When you turn a ceiling fan off, it doesn't stop rotating that second. It winds down. The moment you begin to understand your mind, it doesn't stop. Witnessing mind, you can allow it to slow down, and eventually thoughts will stop, because they no longer serve you. Meditation is beyond rational thought or even scientific investigation. Our primordial nature is unconditioned, pure spirit. The thinking brain is powered by unconditioned space."

I said I often try to resolve doubts by thinking about them, and Channa suggested, "Don't take doubts personally. Just witness and allow them to be on their way." Since then, I've found witnessing to be a comforting and grounding practice. Sometimes, I even pull over while driving, find a safe place to stop, close my eyes, and feel what's present.

When confusion, doubts, or denial arise, I acknowledge them and try to see their value. There are always lessons to learn. Staying present with each state of mind and body without running toward distraction, we have a chance to bring the opposing voices into an arrangement that pleases our soul. When I stand steady in the face of these energies, I feel peace within. Even when mind and body feel distressed, the soul is fine, and as I enter unconditioned space, then mind, body, and spirit dance as leela, the universal flow of life.

We are souls walking around in human bodies. We can be aware of each difficulty or disease we feel, whether a cold, back pain, or whatever, and try to see it as the soul's attempt to wake us up and get us back on track. Although stresses and struggles might feel as though they arise out of nowhere or are someone else's fault, they are always the soul's attempt to bring attention to something not yet awake. It's best to examine our feelings with unconditioned acceptance and space.

If someone disturbs me, it's almost never about them. It's a chance to discover something about me. In situations I thought I'd already resolved, if an emotion like anger arises, new information is presenting itself and I try to witness. With beingness on my team, I can put all my weaknesses and transgressions into perspective and notice the many fine qualities that surround them. The biggest challenge is not to combat my own tendencies or those of my parents, ex-partners, or friends, but to learn from these messengers without punishing anyone. Like the Saturday morning when I was practicing yoga at home in our little town-home in Melbourne. Mike was downstairs in the kitchen making breakfast as he usually does and the kids were upstairs playing in their room. My mind must have been all over the shop because, as I looked out through the window at the car from where I was practicing shoulder stand, I was thinking how interesting it is that I still manage to walk to the passenger's seat thinking it's the driver's seat. And how unconscious yet conditioned my mind is to still do that even though we have been living in Australia for a few months now, and I know the steering wheel is on the other side of the car.

While I was off musing about this I should have been focused and breathing into the upside down shoulder position that I was in. But instead I came tumbling out and hurt myself as a result. The kids were pretty loud in the background, and Mike's break-fast making was also filling up the sound waves. But was it be-cause of them that I had fallen? Was it my fault? Essentially of course, but as I looked deeper into it I realized that it would be easy to blame the many distractions around me, and I could have even blamed myself for not being more self-aware. But the truth is it wasn't my kids playing loudly in the background that made me fall, nor was it Mike's kitchen noise, and if I was honest with myself, I really couldn't be hard on myself either. The mind is going to wander. That's what it does. It's a fantastic tool and it needs space so that we can use the tool, but not get used *by* the tool.

I learned that day how important it is to not blame my mind, nor anything my kids or Mike was doing. Afterall it isn't about them, instead it is a chance for me to discover something new about myself. Perhaps a shoulder weakness, or how in not being fully present there is a tendency to move down the rabbit hole of the mind and put myself at risk. And if I could be distracted in a yoga position, I might too be distracted with other things in life like how I relate to my loved ones in certain situations. Now I just take note, and see distractions as something to watch and witness rather than to be hard on myself or make it more than it is. Being aware does not mean our mind won't still wander, but it means catching it when it does. Being aware when our minds wander brings us back to the moment where everything is happening for us and in real time.

Proportion

When Mike, Leela, Charlie, and I were living in Australia, when I drove the kids to school and couldn't find a parking space (and was running late), I would park a couple of feet into the crosswalk to drop them off. One day this guy started yelling that I was endangering the children, and instead of responding with humility and respect, realizing there was truth in what he was saying, I plummeted into reactivity. As soon as the kids were out of sight, I yelled that he ought to mind his own business. I don't think I said f-ing business, but in my mind I might as well have! I told him how terrible he was to yell and call me names in front of my children, that his words were worse than parking a little into the crosswalk. I just couldn't let it go! I was back in primary school being bullied.

I marched to the orders of my ego instead of forgiving myself, or him. The next day I got Mike to come with me, and as we dropped off the kids, we looked for the guy to have a few words. Mike grew up outside of Boston, and although he dislikes confrontation, he knows how to deal with testy situations. I felt supported by him, but at the same time, it didn't feel right. I had taken it to another level, and when I eventually got to class at the yoga center that day, Channa told me to forgive myself.

I couldn't see why he said that. I thought the other guy needed to beg for my forgiveness! My ego was raging, and not the compassionate side of my beingness. By reliving past pain, I was creating something bigger. My body felt contracted, including places I hadn't known existed. As I forgave myself and connected less to the past, I could feel the guilt leaving and I stopped tensing my organs.

As I continue practicing with Channa, I realize how important it is to take time each day to pause and reflect. When I don't, tension accumulates and spreads. Practicing steadily, when Mike's and my coffee runs out, the milk spills, the wi-fi sputters, or the children are defiant, I'm less reactive and irritable, and more patient. Life flows.

These challenges look trivial, like "first-world problems," but without a steady practice we get bogged down by them. When situations like these arise and we're in unconditioned space, we're less reactive and able to imagine solutions, or at least let the water run off our backs. In unconditioned space, I recognize these challenges as gifts that can help me be more present, and I might choose to drink tea instead of coffee that day, or apologize, or take a few moments to connect with my kids. I might even help them tidy their room so they see how deeply I care and that I'm trying to be awake to what's important and not blow situations out of proportion.

When something feels uncomfortable, we need to be careful we don't just run away or try to change what's happening. We can become addicted to peace and hold onto it. My soul wants me to be in the flow of life as fully as possible. Kindness arises from spaciousness. When impatience builds in me, it means I've stepped away from who I really am. Many things will go "wrong," but when I forget who I am in the midst of adversities, I only hurt myself and those around me. Being impatient takes the joy out of life. It's important to connect with our primordial nature and experience the fullness of all that's real.

Precious Human Birth

One day after yoga, Channa invited a few of us to stay behind and enjoy some of his incredible Sri Lankan dishes left over from a cooking class. One student expressed profound gratitude for

Channa's teaching. Channa replied that all spiritual knowledge is meaningless unless we can love all that's happening in the moment, with a soft heart. Reflecting on a book he was reading at the time, *A Path With Heart* by Jack Kornfield, Channa told us, "Even the most exalted states of consciousness or the most exceptional spiritual accomplishments are nothing if you can't be happy in ordinary moments and if you can't serve and touch one another."

What matters most to me now is whether I'm living fully just like Jack Kornfield mentioned in his book. If my life ended today, could I leave without regrets? When my time comes, I hope I can say I've lived my path with heart. Before receiving and practicing these teachings, my perspective was so limited. Now I try to release from the tentacles of my small mind and be grounded in my heart. When I do, I have no regrets. But the mind is strong and without living in awareness, envy and other hurtful tendencies can take center stage. When I take the time to witness whatever's present, dramas and tensions lessen. Shining light on confusion, feeling the breath move in and out, the mind becomes more at ease and the body and heart center return to running the show.

I usually practice in the early morning, but any time is good. Sometimes, when my mind is running amok, I pretend it's an unruly child making up stories or saying things that aren't true. As soon as I begin to witness my mind, it defers to heart and body, its wiser siblings. With patience, reason, and love, challenges become lighter.

Before I began this practice, when there were difficulties in our family, I'd try to smooth them over. Now my main practice is to witness, allowing Mike, Leela, and Charlie to be themselves—to complain or do whatever they need to do. Simply witnessing encourages them to become aware of themselves and to express their troubles. I don't chime in, I just try to hold up a mirror. It is a practice though and I wouldn't say that I've mastered this, but I do know that I'm doing my best.

Everyone needs to find their own answers when they're ready, and it's best when I don't interrupt the process. Sometimes I'll suggest options, especially for the kids when they're going through something. I don't ask them to change, but I offer other ways to look at something. After I'd been practicing with Channa for a few months, it became easier for my kids and husband to be around me. I stopped living from a place of lack and a need to fix everything.

Now when my children ask questions, I answer truthfully but only within the scope of their inquiry. Channa says the best thing we can offer our children is to allow them to grow in the way they're meant to. They don't come into the world conditioned—that comes from parents, caregivers, and society. As I take this in, I'm able to forgive my own parents and forgive myself for my part in my kids' conditioning. My parents were gifted to me to learn and grow from. By having this practice as a constant reminder of truth, I do my best as a parent to Leela and Charlie.

There was a time when Leela was having trouble with some of the girls at her school. I just listened to her, not saying too much. Suddenly she looked brighter, as though she'd found the confidence to deal with the things she was going through. I think she was able to see that I trust her to handle her nine-year-old life herself, and that things don't need to go a particular way. Acceptance, listening, and witnessing are healing for everyone. A deepening of consciousness is the only way for us to truly grow, and it's easier when we feel truth for ourselves through our own experience.

Accepting both my children and my husband for who they are is important. Everyone wants to be accepted for their own truth, and not who they feel they need to be for our approval. When I feel acceptance within *and* from another being, deep love is actualized and conflicts resolve.

When we place nonacceptance and acceptance in a steady stream of compassionate awareness, it can be transformative. When we're undisturbed and deeply inside unconditioned space, tears may flow, touching the core of who we are beyond human form, yet also very human. This is something to experience and to celebrate! Being born human and living and breathing as spirits are gifts from consciousness.

Channa told a student that he could have come into the world as any kind of consciousness—a fly, a piece of wood, or any of an infinite variety of forms. No offense to all the incredible wood and beautiful trees in the world. They are the very breath of life. But this made me ponder how incredible it is that I incarnated as a human being this time around. I don't want this gift of human consciousness to be in vain. By the very act of writing this book, I'm sharing the immense delight of being of service, and I'm thankful for the opportunity. We each have the opportunity to be of service however it presents itself. Through the daily practice of living in awareness, I feel capable of staying present with myself and living my life more fully.

CHAPTER TEN

Intuitive Intelligence

We're all born with instincts, an intuitive understanding that arises from sensations often felt in the belly. Societal pressure and conditioning have moved us away from this innate way of knowing, but science today recognizes "gut intelligence"—called *dantian* in Chinese and *hara* in Japanese—as our second brain. Meditation helps us connect with this intuitive intelligence. When I feel connected to my gut brain, I glimpse things otherwise difficult for me to understand. When my mind is at rest or when I'm practicing witnessing, I can feel my *body's* intelligence move to the forefront of consciousness.

Channa, two other students, and I were in the yoga center's tiny kitchen. One of the students asked Channa if it's possible to *witness* multitasking. Channa replied that living in awareness means being present on all levels with all realms, and can be practiced anywhere, including in the kitchen. "When I'm cooking, chopping, chatting, and planning next week's retreat, awareness is possible. We can be conscious of more than one thing at a time, but without the practice, we're often aware only of the mind's fluttering. With cultivation, we can deepen our awareness to include what's going on in our body and many other realms."

On another day at the café, Channa told us that most people live in their minds. "If you don't practice meditation," he said, "it's like being a fish and not realizing you're a fish. Then one day you're pulled out of the water." That was me—dwelling in my mind and not knowing it until this practice pulled me into deeper awareness. I now know that all beings are a part of me. We share the earth as our home. Knowing this, we can build and heal all communities, inner and outer. When sensitivity and vulnerability are celebrated and we relate deeply to one another, isolation is a thing of the past. Interconnectedness goes beyond the mind. Cultivating intuitive intelligence becomes a way of life.

Before meeting Channa, I spent most days identifying with and then reacting to my thoughts. It was exhausting, and even today, I feel the effects of decisions I made before having the tools of living in awareness. Practice allows me to feel connected to myself and our Mother Earth and be able to access the beauty of each moment. With this way of being, I can stay connected with the intuitive awareness that supports my life.

Until practicing with Channa, my heart deferred to my mind. I thought I was leading with my heart, but now I see I was acting out of ancient patterns that weren't in my best interest. Like how a hug can be just another thing we do, or it can be the most wonderful exchange of energy between two people. When we hug someone we have the opportunity to feel into who this person is and the many good qualities they possess. In that very moment we send loving energy from one heart to another and not just for the sake of appearances or out of habit.

All dualities are born in the mind, and beneath that is the depth of absolute oneness of being, what some call God, nirvana, or samadhi. If our experiencing is not through this deeper awareness, it's dualistic and ultimately leaves us unsatisfied.

I used to think Australians were the best people in the world. Studying with Channa, I realized this was a false idea that had arisen in the duality of my mind. There is enough room in our hearts for all countries and cultures and all the colors of the rainbow. The mind can be limited to two dimensions. Whatever we see through the mind's eye becomes black or white, good or bad, right or wrong. Channa told us one day that before light enters a prism, it is one ray of white light. Then it becomes refracted, and the one becomes multiplicity. Is this why the world is populated by talking heads and split realities—because the mind is a prism and our being-spirit is a white ray?

We never have just one *mind*. Although mind and brain are not identical, for the moment, let's focus on the brain's two hemispheres. The right hemisphere is linked with the left side of the body and lights up when we are creative, spiritual, intuitive, inspired, inventive, or mythopoetic. The left hemisphere is linked with the right side of the body and is activated by rational, logical, linear, factual, mathematical, or scientific mental activity. Sometimes these aspects seem to be competing and we feel we need to choose just one. But we can engage the whole brain.

In deciding where to plant a tree, for example, a gardener's aesthetic sense might suggest a place along a hillside, while her scientific, problem-solving abilities recognize another place that would be more conducive for the plant to thrive. Appearing beautiful to the eye and the way that satisfies us is important, but we cannot overlook the plant's well-being. A holistic approach will embrace both, finding a place the tree will thrive while enhancing the landscape and feeling beautiful to passersby.

Intuitive intelligence is different from *knowing* something. It's different from *facts*. We sometimes protect our identity by knowing things, avoiding uncertainty. Living in awareness, we become comfortable with *not knowing*. There's no pressure to make the moment into something it isn't. In the past, I'd make demands on the moment by not trusting that things were okay as they are, even when they were so messed up. I needed to know what would happen next, and that often meant going from one relationship to another without giving myself time to just be with myself. I orchestrated and created a new love partner again and again who would fit my story that I wasn't good enough, and needed love from the outside to prove my worth. The love that

I wasn't giving myself was then given to my partner where I eventually leaked energy and felt drained.

We are all so powerful like this and if we demand things to be something different than they are, we have to be ready for a possible fallout and a lesson that comes with it. Just look at the word "fallout." To me it could mean we "fall out" of the flow of what life is already giving us and wants us to pay attention to. And when we demand something we might get confused and say to ourselves that we are manifesting, whereas true manifestation requires that we let go of the outcome, and go on with our everyday life without having to worry about it all the time. When we demand something to be different than it is, we are essentially lying to ourselves and creating less than ideal conditions for healing the root cause of pain. At times even knowing all of this, my ego still cries out for certainty, and when it does I'll try to stop and look at all the energies at play. When I choose a one-sided point of view, I'm not being fair to myself and might cause myself or others harm.

With intuitive understanding, my perspective widens and doesn't require as much reasoning. There's a feeling of trust. Then, when I add reason, a great marriage is born and *beingness* is felt in human form. Having an idea based in truth and at the same time a strong feeling about it, is most helpful. Channa is gifted in this area. He could support himself as a clairvoyant—his sixth sense is that developed—and he uses it for others' well-being. Having this gift, I believe, is a huge responsibility for him, yet I've watched Channa see someone's future and then, in a light-handed, indirect way, gently offer appropriate teachings.

He uses his gift in other ways too. As soon as something heartbreaking happens to me, he seems to know and shows up without being asked. This happened in Australia and continues to happen since I've returned to the US. The Buddha said that if a person gains miraculous powers without having a spiritual practice, he might use those powers to move *away* from the spiritual path and, consciously or unconsciously, misuse his gifts for worldly gain. Channa teaches from a grounded place, living in awareness himself, so others can benefit from the miraculous power of his deeply felt intuition.

The Horizon of Our Being

One day in class, Channa taught that a conscious person can never steal. This is because it wouldn't be *conscious* to do so. As I began to understand the practice, I realized it has a huge moral component, that it's critical to have a foundation in ethics and honesty. Interestingly, I've noticed that when I need or wish for something, it comes in its own time and never in the way or time frame I'd envisioned.

When I was fourteen and wagging (playing hooky) from school, I'd go "shopping," really shoplifting, at a small boutique store. I hated my desire for the cute tops, hats, or dresses that other girls were wearing. I had some money from my job at the Eagle Heights Café, but nothing was enough for me. Was this why a man twenty years older than I was entered my life—to underwrite my desires? We need to be careful what we wish for; it might come true.

I stole many items of clothing, and one day I got caught. I'll never forget the shopkeeper's face. When she saw me put this cute little hat into my school bag, she didn't seem angry, just disappointed in a kind, loving way. With that look, she held up a mirror for me to see myself, and I didn't like what I saw. Time stopped, and I was granted the opportunity to choose the direction of my life. I dropped the hat and ran out of the shop as quickly as I could, feeling shame and remorse in every cell of my body. Getting caught woke me up. I don't think my grandparents or my mum ever knew about this. Perhaps Mum did.

Looking back at this thirty years later and hearing Channa speak of stealing as something inherently not conscious, I see I was caught by desire and living in my smaller mind. The craving for things to fill the void in me and the desire to have others "respect" me because I had nicer clothes drove this whole criminal enterprise. To live consciously, I now witness my desires without acting them out. I can't remove them, but I can watch them and keep them from growing.

My happiness today comes from the connection I have with my true self and heart-filled practice. While meditating in the space of oneness, my desires are often revealed to me. I witness and allow them to be there, while focusing on my breath and sensations. Happiness, for me, comes from not acting out of self-ishness. If we all practiced meditation, we might live in a world where we don't just tolerate each other, but cooperate, recognizing others' needs as important as our own. The greatest gifts, for me now, are being connected to my heart and soul and living who I really am.

Channa's classes emphasize breath and a flow of postures, and he also holds space for us to cultivate reason and make sense of what we're learning. We focus on *the feeling body*, letting the mind stay in non-doing mode to nurture intuitive intelligence, but we never abandon the left brain or reason.

The Unmanifested

As my meditation practice continues to develop, I've become more sensitive, feeling things without being told. I can tell when my kids are having conflicts at school and whether they've been resolved. Looking at their faces helps, but even when they say nothing or just a few words in kid code, I can get to the bottom of things gently and help them through situations they're struggling with. I can see the benefits of practicing living in awareness in my children's lives. As they are embraced by the truth, it frees them to be themselves. In a good moment when I'm being mindful I don't tell them what to think or feel or do. I just try to surround them with love and compassion, and offer guidance when asked directly or indirectly. This extends to my husband, too. When he tells me a little of what is going on at work, I'm usually able to understand who has his back and who is against him. All my life, my intuition has been pretty good; now I see it can be cultivated by living in awareness.

Sometimes when confusion arises, I'm caught off-guard, unable to remember the resources at my disposal. So without trying to fix anything, I try to be okay with what is, having faith that what has occurred is for my benefit and that I'll find my resources when I can. When I'm feeling into my body and being mindful, I don't try to understand the why's. I just sit with it and remind myself it's okay not to know. With trust in the unknown, the need to manipulate or even fix things vanishes. Divine consciousness is my pilot, flying me into unknown territory, without my knowing the flight plan or the destination.

With this newfound trust in the unknown, I no longer lose myself out of fear or trying to control my direction. If something isn't going according to plan or if I feel confused, I take it to mean that I'm not supposed to understand at that moment, and maybe I'll never understand. Usually it's just that the next message hasn't presented itself clearly enough for me to get it. I allow the wheel of life to spin without adding anxiety or negativity. Self-containment allows for witnessing and acceptance. Receptivity opens me to inspirational messages. Sometimes I've noticed that while there is so much in my sphere that's available to me, I can sometimes close myself off to receiving. This is why making space to be quiet, even just for a few minutes, can be so helpful. Sensitivity became my new norm once I realized the importance of carving out a certain amount of time to be restful and reflective each day.

Our lives are full. We're busier than ever and under more pressure. Many people interact more with computer screens than with other people. With all our devices, we don't always have time to enjoy ourselves, our families, or friends. When we get back in touch with the simple things in life and have the discipline to balance technology with other needs, we weave the old and the new and reap the benefits of modernity. Sharing quality attention with loved ones—at family dinners, for example—is priceless. Taking the time needed to replenish ourselves feeds our soul, and our soul elevates our physical form.

I take breaks from screens, especially before going to bed to ensure a good night's sleep. I feel confident that if there's news or important information I need, it will get to me. Spending time in quiet helps me experience life through a clearer lens, positively affecting my sense of the world around me. Channa says the twenty-first century is the time for us to evolve spiritually. Many of us sensitives are affected by other people's words and actions. When we're spiritually attuned, we can take in the *essence* of their communication and not just their words or actions, opening our intuitive intelligence and inner guidance.

When I witness myself from the horizon and am not just in identification with who I think I need to be, I feel connected to all beings and dwell in unconditioned space. When I live within the constructs of my mind, I remain unaware of who I really am and vulnerable to both the winds of change and other people's opinions. It's crucial to distinguish what's real from what's contrived by the mind—our own or someone else's. When we're able to witness thoughts in their embryonic stage, we can have a better sense of what they are and what they aren't.

I used to think if I could just wrap my head around a problem, I could solve it. In truth, my heart and feeling body need to inform me. The first few months I studied with Channa was like a detox. I had headaches and felt like I was going through a deep healing. His classes were about *experience* and *non-doing*, and finally my mind was able to fade into the background to be used as a tool when needed but not to demand attention all day long.

One day after class, Channa said that *thoughts* are neutral. They flow like rivers with countless tributaries, but they cannot analyze data or make judgments on their own. It's the *intellect* that does that. The intellect acquires knowledge, interprets feelings, and solves problems. Combined with *awareness*, the intellect organizes our responses and helps us manage them in an organic fashion. But when the mind is in "go" mode, thoughts run amok and resting isn't an option. *Witnessing* helps calm the intellect's energy.

For this practice, we close our eyes, breathe in and out slowly, and notice the activity within our minds. We witness whatever is present, and don't try to push anything down. The mind likes to learn new things, but *not-knowing* can be even more helpful at times. "Breathing in, I feel what has manifested (form, doing).

Breathing out, I feel the unmanifested (formless, being)." When I practice this, the exhalation helps me relax into the moment and I feel a great expansiveness. With that stability, I'm able to act on decisions that come from the horizon of my being. This can be called *being-mode*. When we're in being-mode, our *heart* and *emotions* balance the intellect, and life flows.

The other side of the coin of intuition is higher consciousness—divine guides that watch over and protect us. The more conscious we become, the more we feel these beings offering us protection, and trusting in this sense of the "unknowable," we swim in the stream of our life. We're not separate from each other or from many other dimensions of beings and consciousness. We find healing everywhere, including in others' life stories. As souls, we're all on the same path. As humans, we go through pain. We eat, breathe, and bleed the same. It's in higher consciousness that I realize how connected we are to one another. In this truth, self-kindness and self-compassion are the only paths for me to take.

Each difficulty is an opportunity to learn and grow. When I gently hold the voices that are in conflict, resolution can come. Being quiet for a while inside unconditioned space allows me to feel a deep connection to my intuitive intelligence and to make decisions from this place. I feel this inner knowing in my body. It's not a thought, yet words may come in to guide me, and the more I trust my feelings and sensations, the more clearly I see where I need to be and how things need to go in the moment.

This has happened to me many times, but let me give you one fun example, since you're here with me inside of this book. Once I was laying down on the grass having a quiet moment with my eyes closed and my arms and legs spread open wide. I wasn't sure if I was really ready to begin looking for an editor for this book. I had finished writing a version of it back in 2016 but I had never written anything big like it before. So I was musing about what my next steps might be to have the book professionally edited and hopefully published. Out of nowhere I heard a voice inside that said "Wayne Dyer." The voice repeated it three times slowly and it also added the word "editor." Wayne Dyer is an best-selling American self-help and spiritual author and one of my first teachers—I would listen to him while driving around in my car when I was teaching yoga and going from class to class in crazy LA traffic.

I had no idea why I was hearing his name as I rested outside, but I got up anyway and went straight to the computer to find out. As it turns out he had mostly just one editor for decades and I found a contact number for her over the internet—a public radio station where she volunteered. I called the number unsure of what I was going to say, and when a gentlemen answered the phone, I told him that I was "guided" to get in contact with Joanna Pyle and asked if he might be able to give my information to her. She did end up contacting me through email and although she wasn't able to take on any new clients, she did read parts of my manuscript and encouraged me to get it completed. In that same email, she included the poem "The Guest House" by Rumi and said she was moved by what she read in my story. She also said to let her know how I envisioned she might help me.

I was almost jumping out of my seat as I read the email. The thing is, in that moment she had already helped me just with her generosity of spirit, and she provided me with a huge confirmation that I should trust my book journey. To say I was touched would be an understatement and I took it as a sign from the universe that I was on the right track. I still to this day refer to her letter that I saved and when obstacles arise I know it is a gentle reminder of the power of intuition.

This source of strength dwells in each one of us and we can practice it on small things at first. For example, if we're at the supermarket, we can try to intuit what apple feels like the best one to pick up. Once home with this apple, we can discern whether our feeling was correct once we eat it. Or if a long lost friend suddenly comes into our hearts, maybe it's time to pick up the phone and have a chat, or to imagine that they are simply thinking of us at the same time we are thinking of them, and send them love. Intuitive intelligence is available for all of us to utilize; it's a gift from consciousness that, like anything, gets stronger with practice.

CHAPTER ELEVEN

Being with Self and Others

After working in Melbourne for a year, Mike was rewarded for his excellent work with a trip to France. He and his team had reached their sales goals, and his multinational company flew 250 employees with their spouses from around the world. It was like winning the lottery, again! We stayed in a luxury hotel in Paris's first *arrondissement*, and I pinched myself—*Is this really happening?* We were bussed to gourmet cooking classes, attended a Keith Urban concert at the Louvre just for Mike's company, and I remember feeling as though I'd died and been reborn in someone else's body. Coming from a humble yoga center a few days earlier, where significant personal growth was becoming my new normal, here I was enjoying all the luxuries of the world. It didn't seem real!

Shortly before we left for Paris, Channa shared with me a vision he had of a yoga studio I would build and operate in the US. Channa had never seen my home, yet at a breakfast gathering at the café in front of others, he said, "I see your studio, Mellara. It's in a backyard with lots of purple flowers." I was blown away and told him my backyard is filled with lavender! I dreamed of having a healing center since my first teacher training at the Center for Yoga. It was really in me, but I didn't know how to make it happen, let alone when. I needed to enter the practice of living in awareness, have a relationship with truth and love, and feel compassion for myself before offering lessons in these things. So when Channa said this, I was ready.

In Paris, feeling on top of the world, sitting in our grand hotel room, I decided to tell Mike. "Channa sees a yoga studio in our backyard. I'd like to name it Dassanayaka Yoga, Channa's name, same as the one in Melbourne. We have Channa's blessing." It was the first Mike heard about this. In my exuberance, I'd lost touch with his needs and the pace at which to tell him, and to genuinely include him in the decision. Mike reacted emotionally, then covered it with reason. He said he didn't agree to build a yoga studio in our yard, and certainly not to name it after my teacher. We'd have to do market research, he said, finding his composure, before coming up with a name. Just saying it's going to be called Dassanayaka Yoga is not a wise way to proceed, Mike explained. He's a marketing manager and knows a lot about business, but at this moment he really didn't know what he was talking about. I described other yoga studios named after their teachers, like Bikram and Iyengar, to transmit the heart and practice of the teachings, and I didn't see this as different. So Mike retorted, "It's not *your* name," and I said, "It's not about me. It's about honoring the lineage. With Channa's leadership and blessing, we can serve many people." This was the way I saw things, but Mike wasn't ready to digest it.

Trying to help me see what was to him a bigger picture and to protect both the practice and Channa, Mike added that from a marketing perspective, a name needs to be remembered, pleasing, and include a call to action, not be something that raises more questions than it answers and sounds like a cult. He added that this isn't what Channa's practice is, and certainly not what Channa is about. We left it at that, as we had no plans to move back to the States anytime soon.

Even before I'd opened my mouth, I knew it was too much information to bring up all at once, but I couldn't help myself.

I'd dreamed of having a healing center like this for many years, and knew it could finally happen if I created it with Channa. So when Mike failed to agree wholeheartedly, I felt rejected and split inside. We were on our first real trip together away from Australia, hoping to reconnect deeply, and now it was more of a disconnect. Everything looked bleak, and over the next couple of days, I couldn't enjoy Paris at all.

I was at war within and without, and within hours, Mike and I both got really sick with the flu.

Stress on the body is very hard on the immune system. The long flight from Melbourne to Paris probably opened us up to viruses in the cabin air, and if we'd had a more relaxing and peaceful arrival, I'm sure our immune systems could have kept us healthy. But with the stress of disharmony, all bets were off!

Looking into the future made us both nervous, for different reasons. Mike said I needed to be there for the kids, that having two of us work (he considered running a yoga center work, which I guess is true) would make it hard to raise the children the way we envisioned. I understood his point and earlier would have agreed with him, but as a river runs its course, so does change, and now I felt I could do both. I tried to assure him that the children would always be well cared for and what's important is that they see us as people who follow our dreams, who live our truths, and that if they see that in their mom, they can bring the same confidence into their own lives. Children learn from their parents' actions, not just from what they say. "Do as I say, not as I do" isn't real. Serving my family is my priority, and bringing the practice into our home always helps me grow.

Mike assumed that if we had a yoga "business," we'd run it together, and he felt that doing so would bring workplace conflicts into our home. In my vision, spaciousness and grace would be entering our home too. I knew that by helping others, my voice would become stronger, and I told Mike it would be beautiful to share that with him. I also said I would take responsibility for the day-to-day operations of the studio, that he wouldn't have to do it. It wasn't a matter of ownership, but a way for me to share Channa's generosity. Although it would be structured as a business, the pure intent would be to share the practice.

From the Bible, we get this idea that money is the root of all evil, but that's not actually what it says—it says the *love of money* is the root of all evil. By love of money, it means greed—using money to maintain power, hoard, or harm others. I'm a huge fan of money; not having any doesn't do anyone any good. But we need to even things out, offer more people opportunities to enjoy life, discover their own inner gold, and bring balance and stability to a world locked in survival mode. Money is just a form of energy. It can be used for benefit as well as for harm. I remember hearing Channa say that money is a beautiful thing that allows us to manifest things and be more of who we are.

The studio I dreamed of would be an oasis focusing on the soul's realization, not a place to learn to be like everybody else or churn out new teachers or crunch numbers so hard you forget why the center was created in the first place. I've seen these pitfalls in other studios, and I wanted to create a place so special that beings would enjoy the taste of their own daily existence, show up for themselves, and practice because it's so enjoyable. But that day in Paris, Mike and I were in a disagreement about all these ideas, and I was triggered and blaming him for it. I remembered thinking why couldn't I just let it go and be in the moment. We were in one of the most beautiful cities in the world!

Over time, I came to see that the conflicts I was feeling were inside me, not with Mike. But it took weeks after our trip to give myself the compassion and patience to realize this. In the thick of the disagreement, first I was sad, then disappointed, and finally enraged. I had some awareness that anger was building, but by that time it was already a bullet that had left the gun. I was in a war zone.

With time and reflection, I came to realize that these feelings of rejection and unworthiness are my old stuff that's needing attention and healing again. I could see my ego's need to fill center stage to hide my feelings of unworthiness. And I realized that what we were arguing about was less important than recognizing the way we engaged when we disagreed. It was a pattern that needed healing.

Within the disagreement, Mike expressed a number of valid concerns, but I could also feel the worry and fear in his responses, and I took them on as my own. As this was happening, in real time, I could hear Channa's voice saying, "No one's beliefs can enter you; *a part of you believes what they're saying*, the doubt is within you, not them, and it needs to be looked at and witnessed." Even in the thick of our dispute, I knew it was not about the topics on the table and not about Mike, but about my own wounds and potential healing. What the other person is representing and triggering is the very thing we need to explore more deeply. I remembered Channa explaining that it's easy to see what other people are doing wrong or how they could do things better, but if we placed that kind of attention on ourselves, without judging, the likelihood of finding the truth would increase exponentially.

I said some terrible things to Mike that night, and I regret it. This trip was to celebrate him, yet because my ego felt unheard and unappreciated, I fell out of balance and let him have it. Channa's voice in my head was clear, saying that silence is golden, to sit with it all, and create space, but I ignored the voice and my ego just went off. I felt that Mike wasn't taking me seriously, and I told him so by screaming at him. I was in flight-or-fight mode, having so much to heal and so much to realize.

When I finally began pointing the finger back at myself for deeper inquiry, I asked why I needed Mike's approval so badly. I realized I'd carried this sense of unworthiness for a very long time, and it was time to address it and begin living my truth. In my primitive, unreflective response, I hurt Mike, the opposite of what I wanted. I could have defused the argument and not erupted while still witnessing the conflicted energies in me. But the split cut deep into my heart and with uncontrollable rage, I screamed at him in our hotel room. He yelled back that everyone could hear me, that these are the people he works with, and that I needed to stop! But my ego was crying to be heard, as I was far out of alignment with unconditioned space and the teachings I'd left just a few days earlier. I forgot that peace comes from remembering that only love is real, and that self-compassion and forgiveness need to be practiced and experienced 24/7. Our personal peace and world peace depend on it.

We Are Love

I had been with Channa for about ten months up until this point and still felt that I had a long way to go to understand who I am and who I'm not. I needed the courage to stay present with discomfort and not run away from it. In the days following my altercation with Mike, I felt more vulnerable and finally it became possible to uncover a deeper sense of myself. I could see a pattern that when things get difficult, I feel overcome by dread and do everything in my power to run away. I had to learn to stay with difficulties and allow my love for Mike—and for myself—to be part of my healing. When we stop being in a rush to move on when things get rough, we have a chance to realize what's going on inside, not to blame or shame but to take responsibility with kindness and compassion. Choosing to stay and grow *within* a relationship allows for a deeper experience in each moment. This is living in awareness.

I continued to hear Channa's words in my head, saying there's no life in fear. But I was holding on and feeling angry, and wasn't able to let things be. After we returned back home to Melbourne my body went into a relapse, and I got an infection in my right lung. Finally, after about five days on antibiotics, I had a huge awakening. It was like I was awake but still dreaming, and in this dream-like state, I saw hurricane-force winds inside my body caused by the split I felt inside and with my husband. As terrible as it felt, I knew this image and feeling were massive gifts from the divine that could help me and my relationship with myself and with Mike. I needed to strengthen self-love and self-compassion, and to stay present with this experience. I remembered wondering hadn't I had enough of all of this, and when was I going to just surrender (which is different than giving up) and just be the love that my soul was asking for.

It seemed like an old record playing the same tune for the umpteenth time, yet this time I was finally getting the message. I could see that once I had compassion for myself, I'd be okay with the world and the world would be okay with me. With my eyes wide shut, I could see things in me that were never really me, and I was able to feel and acknowledge the truth of who I am. A molting took place, discarding what was ready to be shed and allowing this realization to remain. I didn't have to do anything about it, I just had to live in the truth of what I was realizing. I felt connected to truth and on the road to healing just by allowing things to be as they are. In this state I felt myself making a difference in the world, and knew if I somehow left the world in this moment I would leave it in a better place than how I'd found it.

Once we returned home from Paris and unpacked, I returned to Channa's classes. At the café one day after class, Channa told us that when we see that we *are* love and strengthen ourselves with this knowing, the outside world will experience positive changes too. It's not that we necessarily go out and fight for peace or for the changes the world so obviously needs, because at the end of the day, that's still another fight. It is saying that some of us might be called to stand up for what we believe in, and it is honoring each of us in our different approaches—there is a place for all of us. Channa said that when your mother's egg and your father's sperm come together, it's an act of pure giving. When the soul enters that form, this realization is a gift to us from the universe, God, consciousness, the divine. Our true nature is birthed from an act of pure giving. When he said this, I felt the undying love I have for Mike and the abiding love I have for myself, and that both these loves are the same, beneath the many layers of conflicts. Sometimes life feels heavy and when it does I try to remember that living in human form is a gift and that every moment is yet another moment to begin again.

I knew I should have let things be with Mike in Paris much sooner than I did, yet I learned a deeper compassion and humility for myself than if I hadn't gone through all of this. The intimacy we have with ourselves directly impacts how we see the world and those around us. Now as I look out from my lens to the world I see it through the eyes of this new understanding and feel grateful to be on the other side of it.

Practicing Peace

"What do we need to undo," Channa asked us in class one day, "in order to allow things to be as they are?" He said, "When the divisions within us are healed, relationships bloom and wars are defused. The starting point," he emphasized, "is courage, to have the courage to explore our patterns and feel them soften as we penetrate them with love." When Channa said this I was taken back to Paris, and what went on with Mike and me. I think the "undo" for me could have been to love myself enough to observe my feelings rather than acting on them as they were only in the beginning stages of forming. Sometimes standing our ground means standing inside of ourselves allowing for an energy of grace to enter, and doing all of that with no one watching at all. The undoing of an old emotional muscle takes a lot of self-observation and deep listening. I made a vow to myself that I would do a lot more of that in the future.

Standing with the clarity of unconditioned space, we're humble by nature and our heart runs the show. This is the way to move into soul awareness. When we're not living in awareness, the smaller mind limits our beingness. When I'm in resonance with my true nature, everything flows in grace, and even if someone close to me is out of alignment, they too reap the benefits of my practice.

Practicing peace and spending time with my teacher, I've had many opportunities to witness my inner dynamics and, at last, to feel much safer inside. I've even learned to speak compassionately to my mum. One time, Leela, Charlie, and I visited my brother in northern Queensland. He lives near Airlie Beach, and our families vacationed together. They stayed at their home, while the kids and I stayed in an Airbnb in town. I invited Mum to join us, but she chose not to. Maybe if I'd asked a few times, making sure she understood we really wanted her to come, stepping into my overly polite persona, she might have said yes. But I chose not to. I just asked her once.

After the trip, she heard how special it was and felt she'd missed out. I told her in my gentle way that I think it's time for her to take responsibility for her actions, or non-actions, and in that moment, I felt a healing energy in the depth of my soul. I didn't know it at the time but this was the beginning of me finding my voice to speak what's in my heart and especially to those who have hurt me in the past. Although my voice was shaky, it was really good for me to get my understanding and truth out of my body. In doing so I noticed a deafening silence on the phone and there was no mistaking the vibration of truth with courage. We didn't speak for a long while after that, yet she was always in my heart as I was finally beginning to realize just how human we all are, and I could see myself in her.

In the past, I would try to fix my mother, to be my mother's mother, and I thought quite naturally that it was my role. I'd play it, and it enabled, perpetuated, and exacerbated the issues between us. That isn't compassion. It's ego, and I was blind to it. I felt bullied and belittled by her, and I gave the same energy back! These patterns helped me survive living in the same household, yet as I look back, they were dividing me within, and from the very person I chose to be born into for greater realization. Now, practicing living in awareness, I'm overflowing with compassion for her.

As a child I was often placed in adult situations either directly or indirectly to be much older than I was, so I didn't get to experience healthy childhood stages like some children do. Being in the middle of my mother's love affairs and holding those secrets close, or taking care of my brother on my own at ten, or being in the middle of my parents' constant wars, it all took its toll. And perhaps another child placed in a similar situation might have fared much better than me. But what I know now is that it matters less what the trauma is, and matters more how the trauma is processed or perceived by its receiver. I grew up fast, and in doing so I need to continue to work with my inner child. It's satisfying work and beautiful to honor just how far I have come. Today it might seem crazy but some of the most wonderful and soothing conversations I have are with my inner child. Because of these conversations, I feel much safer inside of my body, and I know she does too. Because of this work I am able to see myself in my mum, and also feel a deep generational sadness. Perhaps this is beginning to heal through me and my children. I'm starting to realize that I don't need more of that pain in order to heal. I can step back and not react to her, or anyone, anymore. Reacting only makes the situation worse. As a child, I couldn't do this, but through this practice, I see that it's never too late to generate compassion toward myself and others.

Being With

After practicing with Channa for just a few months, I told him how disrespectful my mum had been on the phone during the past weekend. I'd been trying to get it out of my head, telling the emotions to go away, and he said, "That's not what I teach." I was confused.

Channa explained that it's important to witness emotions as they arise and to befriend them, not ask them to leave. Feel them as they come for a visit, acknowledge them without judgment, and hold them close as you would a precious baby. He suggested that I talk with my emotions, take the opportunity not to suppress or numb them anymore, but to feel them as they bubble up to the surface for healing.

As I became more spiritually sensitive, I would take the time to practice this. Sitting quietly in a safe place, I could attend to and release these old patterns of holding. At first the pain seemed to be coming from my mum, but as I looked more deeply, it was clear it was entirely inside me. Seeing how I have been betraying myself, I cried with gratitude and became less and less affected by Mum. As I forgave myself for my contribution and especially for past damage I was responsible for, I began to feel lighter, and a liberating sensation took over my body.

I started to talk to myself, saying things like, "Hello my aban-doned and scared little girl. I see you again, and I'll hold and take care of you." Because these situations first arose when I was a little girl and they entered my body and heart when I was that young, shutting down or getting angry as a child might were the only responses I knew. They were my "normal." Now, living in awareness, I have a golden opportunity to hold that child with love and compassion. I don't wish unkind thoughts or feelings away. I just place awareness around these survival strategies, without judging, and begin to feel much more ease within. It's as though I've discovered an inner locksmith to let me in to the home that is always there for me. For the first time, I became my own healer.

Until all this with my mum started, I wasn't aware of the envy being directed toward me by her or by other students as Channa was giving me hours of his time. Thanks to the practice, I learned not to worry what others are thinking; it's actually none of my business. So I forgave myself and forgave my mum, accepting it all with grace and gratitude, realizing we're all going through sim-ilar lessons. In that moment on the phone, I didn't mention these emotions to her, so I wouldn't hurt her or burn a bridge. I'm still her friend and she is my mother. It's important not to dump our pain—consciously or unconsciously—onto others, as it just keeps the emotional train on track. Not reacting doesn't mean being untrue. It means seeing what's happening and choosing the healthiest response for that moment. Awareness and compassion go hand in hand.

I was finally becoming the Mellara who has always been in-side, uncovering years and layers of conditioning. I continued to witness and stay nonreactive, more settled, and attuned to my senses, and as I did, life got easier. My husband and kids began to treat me differently. Instead of being disrespectful and not knowing why, Charlie awoke to my newfound accessibility and seemed to enjoy it. I was able to listen to myself and others and find my own beliefs and inner guidance. It felt like a long exhale, followed by an inhale into the beginning of a life of deeper awareness. I was living in a healthy way for the first time, and best of all, I know I'm worth it!

Channa helped enormously with my relationship to myself and with those close to me. With a daily practice and a deep respect for other people's conditioning, I could practice compassion and be present with everyone. Before, I had to give my own emotions full attention. When we identify with our persona, we leave the present moment and play oldies but baddies from the jukebox of the past.

Now when I'm being tested, I feel compassion and forgiveness in my heart center, and I can extend this to others, especially those who are there to teach me about myself (i.e., everybody). The person standing in front of me is revealing something unresolved in me that needs healing. I follow my breathing and dwell in quiet awareness. When something in them disturbs me and I find myself wanting to judge or shame them, I stop and witness myself, in granular detail. When I notice an ugly trait in someone or feel uncomfortable around them, I know now that I'm looking at myself in the mirror, and they're gifting me an opportunity to realize something in me that needs attention. *It's never about them.*

How many wars are based on this kind of misunderstanding? When I'm in my mind and not in my heart, it's a kind of war. The energy to scar someone for life begins to course through me. When I was younger, I took many a beating. I was demeaned for the way I ate, the way I was in nature, and harsh judgments and neglect were ways I learned to treat myself. Before entering this practice, I was unable to sail through life's storms. I didn't have the tools. Faux-calmness, faux-wisdom, and faux-empathy didn't cut it. Until I was able to be present with the pain inside, I made myself and others ill-at-ease. Experiencing living in awareness, I'm now more conscious and compassionate in relationships with myself and others.

As a child, when my dad abused me physically yet more emotionally, saying things like, "What are you, stupid? ... You better eat your dinner or I'll take off my belt," I would think, I'm not going to cry, and I'm not going to give him the satisfaction of seeing how much it emotionally hurts. Now I see myself in him and the disconnection we shared. I can love and forgive my dad, and myself, and no longer have an inner dialogue of turmoil and confusion. Only the truth is felt. He was treated poorly and didn't know any better. If he did, he would have been a much different person and dad.

"You Really Like Me"

One time Channa said, "Every little part of our being wants to be heard, and if we don't listen to these feelings, we might need a doctor later to deal with the symptoms. Emotional pain manifests in physical form. We don't need to over-effort, just allow what's there to be there and to convey its message to us, so we can heal what is not yet in harmony." It wasn't difficult to shine the light of consciousness on the ongoing conflict with my mum, but it wasn't exactly easy either. It was a dominating force in me, robbing me of being present. But this time I held the fear lovingly and didn't stay long enough to have to pay for a late checkout.

All the survival strategies I'd relied on before Channa, like being a victim or making myself sick with angst, were still there, but were now in the background and I wasn't indulging in them. I didn't give them the energy I used to. Instead, I was able to witness these states without being swallowed up by them. "What do I do now?" I asked myself. It was engaging and terrifying at the same time, because a new muscle was being stretched. I felt truly alive! Realizing I could heal myself, magic began happening.

I saw that automatically taking care of my mum emotionally was a disservice to us both, and I needed to live my own life fully. Today, when situations like that arise, I remind myself that I'm able to experience anxiety, fear, pain, illness, or whatever it is, and I feel a great embrace from the universe. Loving the unsteady, unlovable parts within myself, I feel whole.

After this big healing, Channa reminded us to be careful about labeling anything as success or failure. It's all, he said, a colorful dance of experiences, an ebb and a flow, not unlike the ocean when the weather changes from one pattern to another. It's our choice if we want the practice to be real or unreal, authentic or inauthentic, alive or dead. For so many years, I yearned for spiritual truth to liberate me from suffering. As I look more deeply into that longing, I see that it's wholeness and a connection to my authentic self I want. Living in awareness has helped me understand the kind of healing I need, and I've stopped adding fuel to the fire. This comes from the deep pool of love in my heart.

Feeling hurt by someone else's actions, I recognize it's not what they said or did to me, but what lessons are in there for me to realize. I always yearned to be free of jealousy. When it comes up, I sit with it and try to love myself more, realizing I've always been enough. I might also flip jealousy on its end and interpret its energy as me being inspired by another. There are so many incredible people in our lives and what a gift it is to realize this, experience their gifts and their achievements in the world. That's always such a fun process and everyone wins. These emotions come in for a visit either for a season or a reason and are usually quite purposeful in our soul's growth. How we perceive and receive them is up to us. We could jump onto them for an emotional roller-coaster ride, as I did in Paris. Or we could breathe, feel into our heart, and witness our feelings' strong emotional and somatic content.

Before meeting Channa, I would try to be perfect in everything. I wanted people to think I was the most truthful, the best yoga teacher, the wisest, so that the wound of not loving myself wouldn't be out there for everyone to see. Another way I avoided allowing others in was by being overly polite. I felt unworthy, like my opinions didn't matter, so I tried to please them to receive a pat on the back. Being perfect or polite was a way to cover up insecurities; it was playing small and unconsciously directing others' attention away from seeing me any other way than how I wanted to be seen, the tail wagging the dog.

Early into meeting Channa, he asked me to show a few beginning yoga teachers what I knew about yoga. I was new to Melbourne and the center, and I felt vulnerable. Feeling this way back then, probably as a protection, I become overly polite. I did it unconsciously, not even realizing the implications of this simple be-havior. With Channa's guidance, I came to see it as compensation for an emotional wound connected to a story of who I am, or rather needed to be. I created and identified with this persona as a small child, when most conditioning is birthed. This certainly was not the real me, and as I started to look at my past, I remem-bered many situations where I got in the way of myself because of it. And it wasn't a question of any lack of knowledge or even wisdom that I could pass on to them, it was rooted in the way I was conditioned and believed was my truth. Carrying the child-hood pattern forward, every decision was about seeking affection and approval from the outside. It's probably why acting and be-ing on stage was so important to me. I truly believed that if I had the admiration of the people around me, I must be a lovable per-son. When Sally Field accepted the Academy Award for Best Ac-tress in *Norma Rae,* she said, "You like me, you really like me!" I could relate!

I dug more deeply and saw the belief that if others could see how polite and perfect I am, there would be no envy, possessive-ness, or other negative traits in me. When Mike would call me out on this, I'd get defensive, believing he was wrong and in tell-ing him so, strengthening my ego even more. If I were perfect, I'd have no blemishes and could carry on in my delusion. Through the practice, it became apparent to me that I'm not per-fect.

In the weeks after this awakening, I grieved the death of this aspect of my persona, and I wondered, can the death of parts of us be harder than physical death? Drama and over-efforting were no longer required. It was a time to witness and be with my own heart, and in the end, I felt as though a heavy weight had been lifted off on the wings of consciousness. When the student is ready, the teacher appears.

Now I finally understand that I *am* good enough, and that who I've been searching for has been there, inside, my whole life. Once I realized this, the blessings were instantaneous, and now I can enjoy each moment simply by experiencing it without feeling the need to be "better." Perfectionism and super-politeness sucked the pleasure out of life; I had to be "on" all the time. The practice has helped me see this persona and simply witness whatever emotions come up and respond with compassion, supporting the journey my soul wishes to take. When we're connected to our whole selves, we see that the whole planet is a part of us and we're a part of everything.

CHAPTER TWELVE

Living in Awareness

When I first tried meditating, there was so much pain in my lower back, I chose not to continue, and did asana practice instead, working on my body posture. I was identifying with the flaws of my body, and practicing meditation was just too difficult. Some days I wouldn't practice and other days I would try to push through the pain, and in the process, I'd only create more unease. I didn't understand that these parts of me needed to be held in awareness—to embrace what was there, as it is, by seeing it honestly without trying to change it.

Now I visualize a child coming to me crying, and I hold her. I don't shake her or ask her to change, I just hold her. When I do this, I feel compassionate awareness and behold the energy of a child within. I don't identify with the physical suffering ("I *am* my pain"), I use it to go more deeply into my inner world. Because of this daily meditation practice, I feel freedom within. Everyone can be a meditator right where their body is today. Because the smaller mind tries to convince us that anything new, strange, different, or difficult is beyond our ken, it can be difficult to establish meditation as a regular practice, like brushing our teeth or cleaning our room. Just by making time for meditation we can build a temple of love in our hearts.

When I lived in Melbourne, I observed Channa taking good care of his body and, at the same time, not identifying with it. Taking care of myself and not identifying with my body or persona are practices I can only do for myself. No one else can meditate for me. I am responsible for my innermost well-being.

There are things we do every day that can be made into a meditation. I find nothing more beneficial, for example, than showering meditation. As I cleanse my body and mind, I commune with my soul. The sensation of water falling down upon my skin and the warmth of the steam against my beating heart is simply blissful. In such moments, communion with my soul, with my beingness, is not separate from communion with the whole cosmos—with all of existence, the divine, the universe, Mother Nature. I use this meditation technique to access my being within, and it takes no additional time. I already shower daily—now I meditate at the same time. The profound quiet of the water pouring down, feeling, hearing, tasting, and smelling all that I perceive in these moments opens me to unconditioned space.

Formal Practice

I have a shrine at home, an area I use just for meditation and yoga. I start each day by gazing at the fresh flower arrangement on the shrine, or altar, and if the sun is already up I look at the place where sunlight has taken rest. Channa told me that gazing at the shrine in the early hours of the day and feeling its energy gives us a glimpse of how the day is going to go. After that, I light a few candles. Having a space dedicated to meditation helps us go more deeply, because our senses are already attuned to the energy field established there and naturally take us within to our feeling body and mind. My shrine is a place where I breathe deeply into my heart.

You may already have a meditation practice that works for you, but if not, here are the instructions I offer my students:

Sit comfortably, either on the floor—cross-legged with a cushion or a folded blanket under your sit bones, or on your heels with knees forward and a blanket beneath you—or in a chair, with your back reasonably straight and your feet flat on the floor. Relax and lightly close your eyes.

Slowly, become aware of your breath, and your body breathing you. Notice the quality of your breathing, whether it's shallow or deep. Neither is "better," you just need to observe it as it is. Allow your awareness to take you on a journey to the breath that breathes life within you. Without breath, we wouldn't be alive as spirits having a human experience. Breathing in and out, over and over, is a gift. Feel your breath entering and leaving your lungs. It's like a bridge between heaven and earth, between the natural world and the room or space you've dedicated to practicing yoga and conscious breathing. In this space, everything and nothing are there at the same time. Inhale deeply through your nose and allow your belly to expand as you do so. Then exhale. Do this for a while to warm up and to deepen your breathing.

After that, hold your breath at the top of the inhale for a few seconds, then breathe slowly out your mouth, allowing the body to completely relax on the out-breath. Breathe in through your nose and out through your mouth six more times, your lower belly expanding and contracting. Are you feeling more relaxed? This way of breathing helps you become more attuned to the breath inside your body, to feel "the body in the body."

Now breathe exclusively in and out through your nose, while slightly constricting the back of your throat, allowing the breath to pass through that thin space called the larynx. Developing a gentle sound you can focus on is important, but not so loud that someone five or six feet away can hear you. It might sound like snoring, or Darth Vader. This is called ujjayi breath. (When I first began my yoga practice, it took me up to a year to understand how to do it correctly. The Sanskrit word "ujjayi" means to conquer or to be victorious.)

As you follow your breath, almost certainly your mind will begin wandering. This is okay and totally normal; we can't turn off our minds. Allow thoughts and images to come in as though you're watching them on a movie screen. But be a witness rather than playing a role in the film. The thoughts that roll in are clouds on the mind's screen. Don't change anything; allow and accept what's there. When you notice you've drifted into thinking or planning, gently bring awareness back to your belly breathing while still breathing in and out exclusively through your nostrils. Try not to judge yourself or analyze what you're doing.

Usually when I first sit down to meditate, either morning or night, my mind is busy. So I witness my thoughts and try not to get engaged with them. I just watch them and bring attention back to my breathing, feeling the ebb and flow of breath moving through my belly. If my mind is still jumping all over the place, I move into alternate-nostril breathing for two to three minutes.[*]

When my attention takes me to a place in my body where there is an ache or a pain, I practice loving this area with my awareness, allowing and accepting that it's a gift for me to learn something I don't understand. It might be an emotion that settled in my body. Most important is to experience it without judgment, simply allowing it to be there with space around it.

Some mornings I wake and my mind is telling me I have too much to do that day and I don't have time for meditation. No matter how I'm feeling, I remind myself that this is a *practice* and I do meditate. Eventually, I begin to feel more settled.

My mind likes to analyze challenges I'm going through, but meditation is not a problem-solving technique. So when I notice my mind doing this, I return to my breathing, my feeling-body, and the unconditioned space I'm in. Before meeting Channa, I used to think of meditation as work. Now I see it as a profound rest for my body and mind. Meditation helps me witness all the

---

[*] For a more detailed explanation of ujjayi breath and alternate-nostril breathing, see "Breathing Techniques" at the end of the book.

contrived stories about myself and others that flood in on a daily basis. I see that they're not reality, just games in my mind.

I continue my meditation instruction to my students like this:

As you breathe in, place your attention on your lower belly. Continue to inhale and bring your attention to your heart and then to your throat. As you exhale, just relax, letting all the breath out before inhaling again and focusing on the lower belly, the heart, and finally the throat. Do this six more times, noticing belly, heart, and throat as you breathe in.

Now notice the places in your body that yearn for attention. Your body might have aches and pains; this is so normal. Observe if your body is releasing tightness or holding on to it. Allow compassion and awareness to penetrate these areas.

When your mind feels restless and wants to stop this focus and go on to something else, try to sustain your awareness on these places for a few more minutes, observing without getting involved. If you need to scratch your nose, instead of giving in to the impulse, witness the feeling and continue to focus on your breath and the tense places in your body. The impulse might dissipate, or perhaps it will get stronger—either way just witness it. Allow your practice to unfold in this way, without manipulating anything. You're the passenger in a vehicle being safely driven by the deep wellspring of your inner awareness. We need to take space like this from time to time to refresh and behold.

Now notice other states that want your attention. Feel them with a deep and kind presence, so you can open and heal these dimensions of your being. The heart and the feelings go through similar processes of healing, and they are assisted when you offer attention to their rhythms, nature, and needs. When you touch your heart in this way, it will begin to open, exposing a lifelong accumulation of personal and universal sorrow, of misplaced faith, of aging, of illness, and of the many times you experienced sorrow somatically as contractions and walls around your heart.

You might also notice other wounds—abandonment, for example, or pain for no apparent reason, so many unshed tears. You might crave something external to distract you from these feelings you never felt because you sensed the shadow of the ghost of it all. Living in fear of this ghost is so normal, and of course as a child, you chose to shut down. To do otherwise was unthinkable.

Now that you're calm, centered, and courageous, you might like to enter into the darkness. Perhaps you feel shame or unworthiness. Memories of early childhood or family pain might be arising, or the feeling of complete isolation, or ancient grief or loss. Take a moment to feel your heart and your breathing. Hearts are broken and shaken to the core. With the support of the practice of living in awareness, you can try to stay present with your heartbreak and open yourself to the unspoken feelings that run deep. Let them move through you while you breathe consciously and stay as steady as you can. Witnessing difficult feelings and sensations moving through you, you can recognize them and allow them to tell their stories. Just watch.

When light and shadow come together in the heart space, our practice is to treat both equally. Everything we encounter can be made to feel whole. Just as when we strengthen the muscles in our body with exercise, a strengthening of the undivided whole takes place when we meditate and practice living in awareness. In the quiet of meditation, our inner light shines on the noble qualities within, and our heart connects with the core of existence. Dwelling on the truth of what is, we're less myopic, selfish, or materialistic. When I practice consistently, everything I encounter feels bathed by the divine.

Meditation doesn't answer all our questions, but it creates space around our inquiries, allowing us to be present when "answers" present themselves. Practicing meditation regularly helps me sustain connection with my heart and to come from that place of wholeness whether I'm on or off the cushion. With consistent practice, my heart becomes resonant, my body able to feel into answers, and my head knows its place and doesn't always just take the ball and run with it.

Some days when we meditate, we'll just breathe and enjoy quiet sitting. Other days, we'll enter the dark and scary basement of consciousness, the pain held in our muscles and bones, the fears and images held in higher consciousness. In all these cases, we just sit and breathe and know that we are a spirit in a human body. To complete our time of meditation, we follow our breathing to calm ourselves and enjoy our newfound stability. It can be helpful to have the guidance and support of a meditation teacher or group or a yoga studio. Sometimes a teacher or a friend in the practice will see things that we ourselves miss. After sitting, I usually move into some stretches to open up my physical form.

The Energy of Awareness

One time at the café after class, Channa talked about the energy of awareness. He said that with awareness, we cultivate a force that brings no harm and is always healing, that living in awareness showers a floral fragrance that reaches everywhere. Awareness keeps our dignity intact and allows us to experience true freedom. The small mind, which is the opposite of awareness, can be a violent force against ourselves or other beings. The life force we experience in the practice engenders gentleness. To bring this into the rest of our lives, we need to track this energy, witnessing when it's present and when it disappears. When we lose our heart connection, it's like trying to live without water. Our true self will perish no matter how perfect our words or deeds may seem. When a sentence like "I love you" comes from our head and not our heart, it's disembodied, and true love vanishes. The heart can rewire the brain, but the brain cannot rewire the heart.

Many of us are planners. What is most important when I'm planning, with pad and pencil, on my iPhone, or in my head, is to do it in awareness and witness when my mind disconnects from my heart. When the mind starts running amok with to-dos, I try to feel what is present in my body and enter the somatic experience without identifying with what's on the surface. What am I smelling? What am I feeling? Is it warm out or is there a crisp chill in the air? Are there sounds? Can I hear the sounds themselves without labeling them or identifying the source? My effort is to keep the mind from disconnected riffing. Planning is important and the cerebral cortex can serve us in important ways. Organizing and strategizing are critical capacities of the mind. But when I do these things in an unconscious way and the mind starts to get out of control, I need to stop, breathe, and return to my heart and my body.

The benefits of meditation are manifold. When I offer my heart and body complete attention, my mind can rest and my soul is nourished. Allowing my mind to rejuvenate, I'm more productive afterward, and able to see from a wider perspective, with no separation. When thoughts return and bombard me like a hailstorm, I can look at them directly without running away and without engaging with them, just witnessing.

When I'm planning or making decisions, I notice whether I'm coming from my heart center or my head. Practicing awareness from the heart allows me to live and love authentically, a stream of conscious intention that trickles into all areas and beings. When I'm in heart-awareness, I'm able to feel my truth, and no matter how good ideas might look on paper, if they don't resonate with my heart, I know it will be a waste of energy to pursue them. I no longer grasp ideas just because I believed them in the past. When I'm that flexible, I suffer less. Flowing in a natural rhythm and not holding onto fixed ideas is calming and centering. Wearing blinders (my way or the highway) does not help.

During one class, Channa said that headaches sometimes arise for the head to be felt. When the mind has been working too much, a feeling of overwhelm may take over. It felt like he was talking to me, as I had a headache that day. So I laid down on the mat and began to breathe into my head and the muscles surrounding my neck, focusing on the breath coming in and out. After a while, I felt some relief and didn't need an aspirin. Being with Channa and the community of practitioners helped me calm my mind and body.

Before moving to Melbourne, I was like a teacher without a practice. I'd always hoped to learn more about meditation, but it seemed too difficult. Teaching yoga postures and teaching meditation are different. I had lots of experience practicing yoga to help heal my lower back. But I realized in Melbourne while studying with Channa that I'm never able to teach what I haven't experienced myself. I was a yoga teacher for eighteen years before I began studying with Channa, and my ego, identity, and self-worth were wrapped up in being seen as a teacher.

With Channa, I began to see that my worthiness didn't need to come from any role. The worth I can count on doesn't come from any identity; we are born worthy. This took me a long time to realize, because the bombardment of my ego was nonstop. It told me things like, "You should be teaching here. Channa doesn't know how many clients you have in America. It's time to let him know." When not witnessed, the ego can be hell!

My ego was raging for recognition. Channa had given me the gift of being a student again and experiencing depths of myself I'm relieved to have found, but my mind wanted a teaching role, a status I'd found comforting in the past. There isn't anything negative about that, but there's more to me than the roles I play.

Early on, I asked Channa, "When will you allow me to teach here, because it's really hard for me not to teach." If I had told him the truth, I would have said, "I find few distractions and your classes help me see all of who I am, and who I'm not. I'm not sure I like what I see. I might prefer distraction, and if you give me a teaching role, I can be distracted more easily. I want somewhere to run, so that I don't have to do the hard work of looking inside myself."

Over time, my inner life became more meaningful to me than keeping busy, and I knew that if I returned to teaching too soon, I would deny myself the time for healing that I so yearned for and needed. Channa never taught us to run away from our roles or responsibilities, but to explore the universe that resides beneath them. For example, family life is a gift with many tests to help us authentically live in awareness, such as having roles without overidentifying with them.

He didn't answer my question about teaching directly, something I became used to, as he rarely answered questions at all. Often after I asked a question, he remained silent, and that alone helped me touch the bigger picture and feel what was behind my own question. That day he said that if he'd had the opportunity to take classes and be nurtured at a center like this, he would see it as a blessing. I received his words humbly and realized they fit. To be an authentic teacher, I needed to be an authentic human being first, and from that depth of heart awareness, experiencing real healing, I could return to the role of the teacher. My ego took a beating—a shedding of sorts—and I liked it. I was relieved of the pressure of being somebody.

A few months before Mike and I moved back to the States, Channa invited everyone in class to feel our courage, reminding us to integrate spirituality into every aspect of life. Doing this, he said, would bring light, wisdom, and compassion into the world. When we act with this awareness, we won't be afraid. What is unknown becomes a friend, and the known is there as a witness.

With a deep reverence for life, I cherish my connection with all beings. Living in awareness, I don't need to be in a hurry, for anything. When we're mindful, life can be a joyous journey, and we can honor our bodies, families, communities, personal histories, joys, and even our sorrows. A courageous heart is compassionate. It is steady and gives us the chance to remain open and responsive to all elements of life, not just the painful ones that try to hog all our attention.

Channa reiterated that the love in our hearts can change the trajectory of self-inflicted suffering. Whatever is present—whether joy or discomfort—we can be with it in our heart space. I realized that no amount of advice, even from Channa, could substitute for realizing this truth myself. When my children were little, I tried teaching them not to touch the stovetop. But Leela is a curious person and went close anyway, almost touching it and feeling its heat. It took her own self-discovery to understand why she shouldn't. I guess she gets that from me!

Going Home

After eighteen months of living in Melbourne, there was a job opening back in California in the company that Mike was working for in Australia. I had a sneaking suspicion that this would be what would bring us back to the States, just as Channa had intuited within those first few precious moments of meeting him.

Channa's intuition was right on—Mike did apply for and got the job, after we all talked about it as a family on many occasions. There were a few reasons why we decided to make the big move back. Even though Leela had made some lovely friends, she was really missing her elementary school friends in California. She also was coming into an age where she was hoping for her own room again and she had her heart set on her old room in California where she grew up. Charlie loved Australia even though he didn't want to move in the first place, and now he didn't want to move back to California. I was in the middle and would have happily stayed yet also missed my good friends and beautiful home and garden. I also think that even though Mike really loved Melbourne and her people, he seemed to have left his heart in San Francisco as the song goes. As an American with more years in America, I think he just simply missed being around what he knew and the San Francisco people.

So the time came for Mike, the kids, and me to return to America, and suddenly I became like a machine trying to accomplish to-do's off a list as quickly as humanly possible. It was exhausting and painful. Then I noticed that when I stay close to my heart, even when the days are full, I never tire.

Even though it was our choice and we were for the most part all on board, I started to feel anxious about all the logistics that needed to be put into place. Our move from California to Melbourne was replaying in my mind, and I could hear Channa's voice in my head saying, "Do these thoughts belong to you? What might be relevant in this moment?" I realized that now more than ever, I needed the support of the practice. So I returned to class after a four-day absence, and Channa gave a talk about dropping from your head to your heart, and simply witnessing the mind. Channa doesn't plan his classes; they're guided from within. He sits in the teaching seat, feels the energy of the room, hears from his guides, and knows what to say, what the class needs. He was aware I'd been unconscious for four days.

As he spoke, tears fell uncontrollably from my eyes, and I realized my addiction to thinking and planning. I hadn't recognized the severity of it. Sitting in silence, listening to his teaching, was healing balm for me. I felt lighter, heart-centered, and ready to tackle our move, calmly.

This was a time, if there ever was one, for me to cultivate the courage I had learned so much about at Dassanayaka Yoga Centre. I would be leaving and would never have access again to Channa in the way I'd had for nearly two years. I had to face my new reality without shutting down. It was challenging, but I knew I had the strength to do it, to practice the teachings I'd learned.

We are love. Devotion to our own being is the cornerstone for everything else. When I realized this, I began to flow and dance inside my life. The devotion I have for my teacher is a projection of the light that resides inside: my higher self. In the past, I put others before myself to influence how I wanted them to think of me. I thought that if I indulged self-love and self-care, it was selfish. What I've realized through the practice is that when I live from the heart, I feel authentic and comfortable in my skin and am enjoyable for others to be around. I naturally do things that enrich my life and the lives of others, and I don't have to manipulate others by acting a certain way. I like myself and like being around others, and they seem to like being around me.

Sometimes in the practice, I feel more sensations and a deeper sensitivity, as though healing is taking place. One day after class, a student told Channa that her body was in a lot of pain. She'd been practicing for a while, and he suggested she be patient because when healing is taking place inside the heart or body, sometimes there is concomitant pain. She said she didn't know what was happening, but she recognized the gift of being in her body after years of living in her head. We all listened attentively.

I could relate to what she was saying. I remembered when I

gave birth to Leela. After twenty-three hours of labor, I ended up having a C-section, and the post-op pain was unbearable. Even though my healing hasn't been like that in this practice, it has been in that realm of intensity. It's not all bliss and serenity. Some days I have sensations similar to that intensity after having Leela, and some days are moderate, while others are neutral.

Channa went on to say that in deep healing, whether it's inside of the practice or any kind of energy work, headaches and emotional or physical pains can bubble up for healing. These sensations in the heart or the body come up to be recognized and released. It could be a past pain that has been dormant, suppressed, or frozen for years or even lifetimes. Inside the practice, if these pains arise, they're there to remind us we're moving into a deeper space of healing. We are processing them on a very deep level.

But it's not the body in the mind. It's the feeling body and heart, where liberation happens of its own accord. Innate intelligence takes over, and gifts inside of consciousness appear when we're ready to open them. When something doesn't feel quite right, we need to check it out. If appropriate, we should see a healthcare professional. Sometimes food can be medicine. Living in awareness, we feel inside the body, and this spiritual sensitivity can tip us off sooner when something needs attention.

Channa says, "This is a practice to *practice*." The mind loves words and explanations which at times can make it harder to practice. He explained, 'When you're hungry, reading a menu won't satisfy your hunger," adding, with a smile, "I'm *very* spiritual. I have mala beads, I dress in a spiritual way, I have brand-name yoga pants.

"To satisfy our hunger, we need to actually eat. If we do and chew carefully, the digestive tract absorbs the nutrients and through the colon removes what doesn't serve the body. When we refuse to feed higher conscious and settle for appearances or toss about ideas, we only ingest nourishment for the mind's lower energy. It's like eating the menu." Most important is experiencing, tasting, and living in awareness.

Everything Is Natural

One cold Melbourne morning as I was arriving at the center to practice, I noticed that one of the students smelled of pot. After class, in private, I asked Channa about it, not as a judgment but as an inquiry, and he told me that no one has to get rid of or stop anything before beginning the practice. He said that with a consistent and nurturing practice and a focused dedication to living in awareness, these things might fall away for some people. For others it may not, as it could be one of the ways they find that works well for them.

He added that everything in the world is natural, and it's not everyone's reality to stop taking certain drugs that are helping. For those who come to the practice wounded, the last thing they need is more guilt. Channa went on to say that this practice does not take the place of receiving help from a doctor or therapist, because recognizing when outside support is needed is also being conscious. When we develop a consistent practice, and as our awareness grows and the connection to the one who is really inside is felt, dependence to substances lessens. What I love most about Channa's teaching is its openness.

When people struggling with mental illness come to Channa for guidance, many seem afraid or ashamed. Not everything can be cured with meditation or living in awareness; nonetheless, Channa's advice is usually helpful. He emphasizes balance. Overcoming the stigma and silence around mental health issues is long overdue.

After nearly overdosing on pain pills in LA at age nineteen, I put myself in the care of a therapist for a few months with that fantastic intern I told you about before. She graduated and moved out of town so I found another therapist who helped me for many years after that. I was depressed, and with my lower back pain, I felt no hope. Therapy helped and offered relief, but many questions remained unanswered. The focus was on improving or changing or putting an end to my problems, and that didn't address my whole body's wellness, including my spiritual well-being. As I look back at the depression I was experiencing in those years, I feel fortunate that I had someone to talk to about it; it provided a good foundation.

I remember Mike asking me when we were first dating why I was smoking pot so much. I told him it was fun, that I was young, and I wasn't hurting anybody else. But I was also acutely aware that I was using it to numb out, to not feel my pain and to have an escape—all valid reasons that I saw modeled to me as a young child. I think I was looking for some more relief and especially at night when things were still, yet my body and mind continued spinning, leaving me feel unsettled. I didn't feel he was judging me, but the look on his face spoke volumes. I think it was, "You're hurting yourself, especially if you don't really need it." Although Mike was well-meaning in his comment, there was obviously something that I was getting in return for smoking pot or otherwise I wouldn't have been doing it as much as I was.

So I ended up consciously swapping out the pot smoking with Restorative yoga and breathing exercises. Mike and I did this together and we often referred to one of my first yoga books by the beloved teacher Judith Hanson Lasater, PhD, PT—*Relax and Renew: Restful Yoga for Stressful Times*. It was successful in breaking up the old habit with something different, something positive and rewarding. It was also something that Mike and I did together as a couple which made it meaningful, and it became the foundation of the love we share today. Our motto back then which still rings true for me is *play together, stay together*. Today Mike and I practice much less together, yet what feels more important is that we have a shared love of yoga and meditating as a daily practice.

All of Me Is Lovable

I have been in pain much of my life, but I wasn't aware of the connection between the emotional and physical constrictions or how they have both been messengers of a deeper message. So, these pains continued appearing in new disguises. When I touched the wound of not having much love or support from my mum or dad, I would blame my partner for not giving me enough attention. When I received rejection after rejection trying out for movie roles, I thought it was something about me—my blonde hair or I was too tall or didn't have enough sass. I didn't have a foundation of self-confidence to see that blaming myself or others was off the mark, that I had deep wounds crying for my attention, that Hollywood producers had their specific needs for filling specific roles, or my boyfriends had their own needs too. It wasn't just about me and what I'd done wrong. Not understanding, I'd just get depressed, berate myself, and feel excruciating pain in my lower back.

I wasn't connected to my body or my heart, and I paid the price. In addition to back pain, I'd get headaches, have sluggish energy, and my heart felt heavy. I remember feeling old in a young body. When I'd tell this to my friends, they didn't know how to help. Yoga practice was my one refuge. In class, I'd be *in my body* for an hour and a half, and it was transformative.

The need to please and be loved was suffocating me, and I took (false) refuge in repetitive, dark thinking. I tend to analyze everything anyway, but I would take it to the next level, overthinking things ranging from what kind of orange to buy, what kinds of activities the kids should take part in, like, everything! Now when I need to decide something, I close my eyes and *feel* into a decision, and I'm okay not always knowing the answer when it hasn't come yet. Sometimes, in that moment, no answer is the answer, and this awakens my intuitive intelligence.

With every failure I experienced and so much of what I cherished destroyed, I'd try to work it all out in my head. Living in awareness, I've learned to witness things much sooner, feel them, hold them gently without pushing or even wishing them away, and accept them. Learning this from Channa, I could finally accept myself and see that all of me is lovable, including what I thought were failures. In the past, I would hide these things under the rug.

The nonstop internal narrative trying to make sense of the emptiness I felt inside began to spiral out of control. My interpretations were delusional, but in those moments, they were my reality—

they were who I thought I was. I thought, therefore, that love was transactional, like "I love you, so what will you give me back?" and I conflated love with lust. Or I'd suppress feelings— "I've been hurt, so I won't go there," creating even more drama. My mind misinterpreted my feelings and created dysfunction.

I thought my fear of being alone was loneliness, and I went from relationship to relationship, and had two marriages that ended in divorce before I was twenty-seven. Feeling lonely even in relationship, jumping back and forth time after time made me sad, but I didn't know what to do. If we think about these things without a gentle witnessing, the belief in delusional interpretations, what I sometimes call addiction to thinking, worsens and transitions into other addictions like drugs, alcohol, shopping, or sugar. Where do these addictions come from? I think they all arise from avoiding pain by trying not to feel it. Deep healing is possible only when we allow our closed places to open. Then it starts to take the shape of space, grace, growth, and surrender. We have to feel our feelings, not run away from them or just meet them on a mind level.

For addictions like alcohol, smoking, sugar, and sex, we have AA and other established safe, healing environments. But where can we go for an addiction to thinking? When I'm stuck in my mind, I turn to coffee, sugar, and fatty foods, and they keep the thinking going and keep me from feeling the pain and constriction in my heart. Living in awareness, I can see what's going on, and am able to focus on the actual issues. We're our best life coach. No doctor can heal our lives the way we can. Once we wake up from conditioning, self-awareness can set us free.

Hurry Up and Meditate

Before beginning to live in awareness, when I felt pain, I would assume it was a repeat of past pains and be stuck. One day I heard Channa say that doing this is like eating stale food. If we can tease apart somatically-retained memories from the present moment and gently allow ourselves to be present, there's no need to do or undo anything. We can hold both at the same time, not denying our trauma, but recognizing that it is not what's happening now. And if we are ready to learn a little more from the buried pain, we have a chance to hear it.

The modern mind is always in a hurry. Slowing down can help the process of witnessing immensely. Lama Surya Das says as a joke, "Hurry up and meditate." When I slow down, observe, and make time for silence (while I witness the urge to hurry), it brings me back into my body and breath, and amazingly helps my lower back too.

In class, Channa told us many people try to stop out-of-control thinking by sleeping or doing drugs. Chemicals, sugars, and fats are attractive because they help us feel better immediately. They disrupt our homeostasis, and for a short while the mind stops. But it doesn't last, and the drug or food becomes the master, reigning over us. We cannot stop the unconscious's messaging indefinitely. It whispers, then speaks in a modulated voice, then a bit louder, and finally it screams in the form of somatic symptoms. All we can do is witness and befriend it, not through analyzing but by realizing this is not who we *are*. When we witness, there's only the river of life flowing in awareness. We live in this moment, as it is, and past and future anxieties remain in the background, or dissolve. This is *samadhi*, the peaceful state in which only witnessing and space remain. Simply witnessing, we move along the river of life in reverence and reverie. Meditation unfolds of its own accord. We only need to watch and not hurry.

Living in awareness is a loving way of witnessing and feeling, and it takes perseverance. The cerebral cortex, developed over millennia, holds the whole of humanity—animals, plants, rocks, and all of existence. To say it's *ours* is not accurate. It's collective; it belongs to *all of us*. As we become aware of it, we see we're not separate from those on the other side of the planet. We are all breathing in and out, feeling our own bodies. Whether we're yawning, scratching, or elongating our spine, as we become aware of it, we enter the stream of all beings over many generations and centuries.

With courage, I work through challenges while calmly centered in my body. To solve a problem, I sit and observe what's present, not to change anything or even find a solution, just to witness. During meditation, when I drop from my head to my heart, my mind becomes less busy and solutions to problems arise from a calmer, more balanced place. When the mind is left to solve a problem, complications based on old excuses and interpretations that are not really my truth are introduced. Now when I witness, I hear my teacher's voice asking whether I'm anchoring myself in thoughts and images, in the body, or in the space outside, and whether I've entered a higher space where ordinary mind can be witnessed.

One time at a breakfast gathering, a student who was about to travel around the world asked Channa, "How do I maintain the practice while I'm away?" Channa replied, "Once you've experienced this space, even if our classes are not within reach, you don't have to blindly accept either your own belief systems or others' opinions, thoughts, or judgments about things. See for yourself what's true. When your thoughts and emotions vanish, when you are in direct contact with the actual nature of mind, then no one's opinions, judgments, or views will sway you.

"Realizing who you are allows for direct perception of your own natural state of mind. You just have to ask, 'Where along the way did it get corrupted?' In this way, you can realize the true nature of consciousness. Spirituality is surgical. When belief systems fall away, when thoughts and emotions of the past subside, what's left is our God-realized true nature, *nirvana*. See beyond your image, or the past or future, or your chronological age. A huge part of you is ageless, beyond time and space."

CHAPTER THIRTEEN

The Spirit of Service

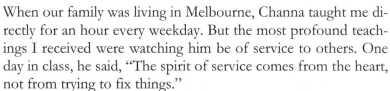

When our family was living in Melbourne, Channa taught me directly for an hour every weekday. But the most profound teachings I received were watching him be of service to others. One day in class, he said, "The spirit of service comes from the heart, not from trying to fix things."

Every morning when I wake up, I go to my shrine and light three or sometimes more candles. The first is for all my teachers past and present, those spirit guides, ancestors, and angels who I thank for what they have done in helping me to realize the divine within me. The second is for Mike and the kids. The third is for the practice itself and for all beings in the world to feel peace and wholeness. Sometimes I light a fourth and even a fifth candle for students, friends, or family members who are going through a hard time. After my prayers I'll usually chant a mantra that is very dear to me and many yoga folks worldwide: *Lokah Samastah Sukhino Bhavantu.* It is a Sanskrit mantra that basically sends out a vibration of sound that translates as, may all beings in our entire world and universe be happy and free. I'm amazed at how this mantra and intentioned healing travel to others.

Then I practice meditation and yoga until the whole house wakes up. During meditation, with the backdrop of the early morning light, I offer prayers to my teachers and all living beings. In those moments, I feel a sense that everything is right with the world and the earth is self-regulating. This ritual reminds me to live from my heart center, connecting with the earth and other planets, noticing and appreciating the breezes, ocean, fires, soil, plants, animals, cars, concrete, and the unconscious that needs our compassion now more than ever. These rituals set the tone of service for the whole day, whether I'm making coffee for Mike and me, preparing juice for the kids, or driving them to school. When we touch the space inside our heart, everything we do and feel throughout the day is infused with the energy of grace and ease. Being of service helps us live in awareness.

Giving From the Heart

Being in the moment is a gift that keeps on giving. I was eight months into the practice with Channa when my daughter's friend came over for a visit. She was sitting quite close to the TV, and I asked her why. She said she couldn't see well. She and her single mum had just moved to Melbourne from Peru. Still learning English, her mother worked as a housekeeper while going back to school to be an accountant in Australia, which is what she did in Peru. She worked hard to support herself and care for her daughter. She also had to pay thousands of dollars of non-citizen tuition for her daughter to attend the same school my children attended for free. I knew this beautiful girl needed help, but not my pity. Nor did she need someone to look down on her. So I walked a respectful fine line to see if she might accept my support. I did some research and found a school of optometry that offered big discounts on eye exams and glasses to foreign students. We took the girl for an eye exam, and she had a new pair of glasses in a few weeks. I had a feeling these kinds of places exist, because when I was an international student in LA with back pain, I found an acupuncture school where I was seen for $5 a session. Doing this helped my daughter's friend and gifted me as well, because I found a way I could be of service and had the wherewithal to act on it.

Channa's generosity is different from most others. He's not a transactional giver, expecting something in return. I saw him give flowers to a student one day, flowers that had been given to him. When the student said he would bring some flowers to the center the next day, Channa replied, "You don't have to. Giving to you is giving to me. That's the essence of giving from the heart. When it feels like the right time to give, that's the best time to." I've also heard Channa say, "Giving to someone else after I've given to you, is giving to me," like paying it forward.

In the West, seemingly altruistic acts can turn out to be sticky. Sometimes our egos are running the show, and we have multi-layered motives. When we come from the heart, our giving is pure. When I was in LA, I saw celebrities give to charities and was suspicious, believing it was more about crafting an image. Perhaps my thoughts were ungenerous, maybe it triggered a question in me about my own giving. When giving is done quietly, not on the donor's timetable but when the recipient needs help, the compassion and beauty of such gifts outshine any recognition the contributor may feel entitled to.

Channa personifies giving for giving's sake. He and Darren helped a member of the Dassanayaka Yoga community who was very ill and didn't have family in Australia. Channa went to her home, cleaned her sheets, paid for her food and medical bills, and took her to the doctor. This went on for weeks. In today's world, this is unusual for someone as fully scheduled as he is. Channa has told me that giving needs to come from a deep realization, that no one can tell you how to feel in your own heart. This kind of true giving helps both giver and receiver realize the importance of generosity. A little help to someone in need can go a long way, and accomplish something bigger than just meeting the particular need. It touches both hearts, which is beyond anything money can buy. The dear soul Channa nursed back to health got better. If it hadn't been for his care, she might not be here today.

While we were on retreat in Bali, a Balinese girl whose father-in-law had died the day before was working in the kitchen preparing our food. Channa offered her the money needed to pay for his cremation. None of the other retreatants knew about this, I just happened to overhear what was going on. A few young adults in Bali have been able to continue their education because of Channa. I've met their families, who are beyond grateful to watch their children live up to their potential. Another time, a diabetic monk called Channa from Sri Lanka. He had only enough insulin to last a few weeks, and Channa sent him the money to buy more. Channa lives from one week to the next, yet he just keeps giving. He takes out loans and pays them back with interest to help people in need. It's moving to me to witness the trust Channa has in life itself.

Generosity

Many of Channa's students love spending time with him, and suddenly eight or ten of us are off to breakfast with him after class. More often than not, Channa picks up the tab for these meals, not because he has a huge bank account or is acting like a big shot, but because his humble heart is moved to make this gesture, and perhaps it's also a teaching for us to learn the values of generosity and exchange. I've heard Channa say that one of the best investments we can make is toward our own awareness.

When Mike and I were about to fly to Paris, Channa asked me to buy a meal for a stranger while we were there. I offered to pay for this lovely young girl, and she almost couldn't receive it, saying, "Who are you? Why would you do this for me?" She looked at me as though I'd escaped from a mental institution. I told her my teacher had asked me to do this and could she please accept it, and finally she did, but it wasn't easy for her.

A Balinese girl who served our food during a weeklong retreat was pregnant with her second child and having a difficult pregnancy. The doctors told her she needed rest and she shouldn't work until after the birth. Before the retreat was over, the woman's husband and her whole family came to Channa to thank him for his spiritual blessings, and gave him their most valuable possession as a symbol of their gratitude. After watching this, I thought, why if they are so poor would they give their most valuable possession? And why would he accept it? Then I realized that Balinese people are very spiritual, that they felt a profound connection to Channa, and for them this offering was part of their own path of spiritual evolution.

After spending a few weeks in Bali teaching and being of service, Channa returned to Melbourne, and within a couple of weeks got a Facebook message from this beautiful Balinese soul saying that the baby was stuck, and to go to the hospital to deliver the baby they would need $500. Channa wired the money, even though he was unable to pay his own bills at the time. She ended up having a C-section and giving birth to a healthy baby boy. My teacher told me that we are beings of service and humanity, and that this life is about service. He added that pure human kindness does not discriminate between self and others, and together we can help any family.

While on retreat with Channa, I heard him talking to Darren about a young Sri Lankan man they had invited into the center to live. He was almost eighteen and about to be thrown out of the home he'd moved into as an immigrant after the huge move from Sri Lanka for schooling and a better life. With nowhere to go, he arrived on Channa's doorstep, and the center took him in.

Channa and Darren taught him how to make his bed and clean the house. He was told not to use the car while Channa was in Bali on retreat, because he was still learning to drive. But the temptation was too great and he took the center's car out one day and crashed into three other vehicles. Even though he said he was beyond sorry for his actions and would pay back every cent, he ran away and no one could find him. Channa responded that this is life, that things like this happen, but we should still give, even though in this case the giving had not been respected.

On my fortieth birthday, a few of us were enjoying a brunch Channa and Darren had beautifully prepared for me. Halfway through the meal, we heard a knock at the door, and Channa said,

"Such a strong knock, this person is in a lot of pain." I answered the door and let in a hard-working schoolteacher who had been out of work for a while. He had a lower back injury and was in acute pain. We all talked a while and offered him a cup of tea, and before long I was in the studio helping ease his pain with a few asanas. I loved being so flexible with my time, very much in the moment, and willing to give. It was a gift to me to see how healing giving can be. I had a chance to help someone who needed compassion and kind attention.

A Spoonful of Love

In the past, I would set aside times on my calendar for giving. But soon I came to realize that going with the flow of giving, when it's needed, is the way it needs to happen. Realizing this has helped me become more attentive, to know when someone is in need, taking into account that something that might look small to me can feel large to someone else. It's important to act in the moment, even when we don't fully recognize the importance of our action for the other person. When situations present themselves, we can tune in to a frequency that's critical for deep giving.

We are spirits in human form, and if we care for her responsibly, the earth will offer us an infinite amount of energy. After class one day, Channa said to me, "I'm giving you everything, like the sun, without discrimination. But if your heart is small and you feel you can only let in a little, that's not the problem of the sun." I started to realize how the mind limits *being*. Whether they're thoughts of not enough money, needing a better job, not having a lover, or judgments based on past experiences, the problem is in the mind, preventing us from being fully in the present moment. Channa was reminding me that I wasn't in Australia to hang out with Nicole Kidman or Naomi Watts, as I'd dreamed of doing since childhood. After that, I never missed a moment to be with my teacher. I was with him like the white on rice until we departed from Australia.

Everything flows in and out, not because it's good to be

generous while expecting something in return, but because being generous serves us and the community around us. Giving comes from the heart, and real giving comes from the depths of our soul. That's who we already are, but conditioning has covered it for generations. Giving for the wrong reasons—e.g., because we want our luck to change—is forced and not true giving. We're all in this together, Team Earth!

While out with Channa after class and at many a café breakfast, I've seen him offer us advice. One day a student asked why money and good energy weren't flowing to her. She had lost all luster in her life, she felt. Channa asked her to look inside and describe what opportunities she'd had to give to others that week. Perhaps a home-cooked meal for the elderly widow next door, or saying hello to the disabled teenager in line at the post office, or the person at work who always has lunch by herself and suddenly you ask if you can buy them a cup of coffee and have a laugh, instead of going straight for your iPhone. Channa added that giving is easy when it's to the people we love, but can we extend it to all our sisters and brothers in the world? He encouraged all of us to learn from nature, and especially the humble bees, who work for years without ever asking anyone to give them a spoonful of love. That is the essence of generosity.

While in Melbourne, my kids and I took the tram a lot, and I loved offering or seeing others give up their seats to those less able. I especially loved my children seeing this. One day I gave up my seat to a child, and in that moment I felt an energy that I'm sure this little boy received—that the world is kind. In small acts like these, we can begin to see that it does take a village to raise a child, and that we're at least a little responsible for each other. I'll never know that child's life, but I saw myself in him and I felt that if I keep treating people with kindness and respect, it will trickle beyond my knowing.

PART FOUR

Waking Up

~

May we awaken from our daydreams, our nightmares, and our thoughts, and witness them instead, experiencing true liberation from within, moving toward the peace that has been waiting for us for a long time.

CHAPTER FOURTEEN

Retreat Yourself

I had no idea what I was getting into. Before going on my first retreat with Channa in Bali, I thought it'd be like the classes in Melbourne, though probably deeper. My intent was to cultivate a deeper awareness of myself. But with the beauty of Bali as the backdrop, and the profound silence, I experienced *the retreating of me* and realized not so much who I am, but who I'm not.

In those seven days, I relived a lot of conditioning that is at the base of the untruths that live in me. My unconscious created this conditioning when I was young to protect me, and it continues to, even though it's no longer needed. I was able to see these root causes of my suffering—anchors of who I think I am—and to leave behind notions that were never me to begin with. I was able to see through and let go of them (or maybe they let go of me). I felt a deeper sense of who I am and became able to live from this truth. It was strong medicine for my healing.

On the days and nights leading up to the retreat, I had been practicing regularly at the Dassanayaka Yoga Centre in Melbourne, and it helped me achieve a deeper understanding of the spiritual path. But during the retreat, the lessons felt stronger and even deeper, and Channa seemed stricter. It wasn't a vacation, but a deep rest and respite from my unconsciousness and ego.

There were nineteen students ready to deepen their awareness and to heal. On day one, we were told not to compare the living standards of the retreat with our homes, but to appreciate the blessing of having this space to heal. We were asked not to leave the retreat grounds, to avoid distractions of shopping, restaurants, or even our smartphones. We were encouraged to have massages, be in our rooms in silence, and take relaxing walks on the grounds. By day two, many of the students were going in deep. For me, it was the silence that helped me move into a higher consciousness and feel answers to many of my questions.

I had heard that Bali is like India in that it shakes you up and makes you just go with the flow. The kindness and humanity of each local person I met were profoundly moving. We were spoiled by their care and service—cooking for us for seven days so we had no kitchen chores, not even dishes to wash. We didn't even have to make our beds or launder our clothes. I felt like a child, or a princess, and I could appreciate the gifts I give my own family by doing this for them every day. Like most parents, we do for our children out of selfless love and don't always realize the impact of the care we give them.

Channa has led retreats at the Nirarta Centre for Living Awareness in Bali for ten years, and he knows that the love built into each brick sings to the petals of every flower. Channa nurtures the staff. He knows the people who work in the garden, cut our vegetables, and bring water to our rooms, and this love accelerates their own spiritual practice. I watched the Balinese people meditate in the early morning before preparing our meals, and as they remove the blocks on their own spiritual paths, they support us all the more. They worked in the gardens and on the grounds as a form of worship, like singing the glory of consciousness. In these love offerings, we experienced devotion in action—acting with knowledge, insight, and sincerity. Channa has guaranteed that we'll experience change on all levels when we bring this kind of giving into our lives.

Before the retreat, Channa blessed the grounds and performed Buddhist rituals to ensure our protection, express respect for the land for allowing us to enter a space of healing, and aid our journeys to enlightenment. Channa has performed these rituals many times, and these selfless acts have created a pond of nectar where we, his students, can quench our spiritual thirst and experience the deeper purpose of life through asanas, yoga nidra, rituals, mantras, spiritual psychology, and the recognition of mortality.

Dance of the Dragonfly

Channa made it clear that we were in the space of the Balinese, not the other way around. The employees, the locals, the sounds, insects, flora, and fauna were there for us to humbly care for and respect their values and culture. This understanding helped us cultivate the strong connection between our own spiritual center and deep respect for all beings. Each day as we entered the beautiful dome-shaped gathering place, candles had been lit, freshly cut flowers placed on the shrine, and the fragrance of Balinese floral incense filled the air. Channa oversaw all those details, assisted by three longtime students, to create a space for us to experience deeper consciousness. As I witnessed my mind becoming content with what I have, and not worry about what I don't have, I became aware of the blessings in my life. I wasn't distracted or on red-alert, as is so often the case. My heart was open and my body filled with deep reverence and gratitude for this experience. At night and during meals, we didn't speak, opening me to the abundance of the natural world. Between dragonfly dances outside my window, crickets, birds, and the center's cow, we weren't in much silence after all, making me appreciate nature all the more.

A few weeks earlier in Melbourne, Channa taught that nature is the essence and core of what we are, and that the five elements of Ayurvedic medicine are well-represented inside us. Particles of earth, water, fire, air, and space all came together to make our human form, and when we die and our souls return home, our bodies return to the earth. So it's easy to feel respect and gratitude for the environment, because we are of the same *matter* ("mother"). Water comprises most of our human form; space allows water the room to move through our organs; air is our energy, *prana*, life force; and soil gifts us food to eat, nourishing us and keeping us healthy. The fire inside keeps us warm and allows the body to move at a comfortable pace, breaking down our food and turning it into energy, so we can live in the ambrosia of our abundant reality.

Nature is our mother, and we naturally and logically give back to her. It's necessary for our vitality—because we are related, because it's the right thing to do, and because it connects us with who we really are. We and nature go together like an orchestra in harmony, ensuring a progression into a masterpiece. This is who we are. It is our home, inside and out.

Homecoming

In the presence of Channa's oldest students, whom I'd met just a few times, I was desperately trying to fit in. I attempted to make eye contact to receive a reassuring glance and feel a part of the group. I said things to gain their acceptance, not realizing I was doing any of this. It was my habitual way of being the new kid in town. I identified with this conditioned persona as normal.

After they left the room one time, Channa said to me—from a place of deep love, yet very sternly, "Why are you trying to get attention? Why are you trying to make eye contact? Haven't you noticed they just look away? They're in a good space, Mellara, why are you trying to disturb them? It isn't pretty, and it's not who you are!"

I was devastated and walked to my hut really hurting. I couldn't stop sobbing; I felt totally undone. My ego kept saying, "You didn't do that! Channa's wrong. Those students are his favorites, and they're all men. He likes men better anyway!" My ego was reinforcing a lifelong story of feeling unrecognized and devalued, and I thought, "It's a f-ing boys club. You didn't do anything wrong. Do not feel bad about it." I was separating myself from the group, a longtime defense, but I knew in my heart that isolation moved me not just away from the group, but away from the truth. My ego wanted to stand up and tell Channa he was wrong, as I had done many times in the past. My lower back began to tighten and I couldn't move well. I felt locked up inside.

After a while, the rage transformed into huge crying, and I began to remember that when I was a little girl I did the very thing Channa called me out on. I saw how much I do this and that the persona I developed at such a young age came from the circumstances of my childhood—moving so often, being dissed by my mum, never having friends for long—and wasn't who I am now. I had been socially engaging and overly polite so many times in my life. When Mum had boyfriends over, I'd vie for their attention, and I remembered her getting upset about it. I didn't even know why I was doing it. Mum was always belittling me, and I lost all respect for her and never looked at myself. I just dished back the hurt, creating a vicious cycle.

I always felt there was something wrong with me, not just because of my mum's dark feedback, but my dad's neglect and abuse too. I thought he really wanted a boy. For years I'd vie for attention and acknowledgment from men and use it to my advantage. In my teens and twenties, these habits just got stronger. After I moved to Hollywood, flirting and other inappropriate ways to achieve love and attention were in full force, recipes for destruction.

After a night of crying and processing all this, I saw that these kinds of things happen to all of us, and suddenly I felt a sense of lightness around my story, grateful to have the opportunity now to look deeply and learn to live in the present and not just in the past. I forgave myself and my parents, feeling profound compassion for all of us. Suddenly, I felt free of this ancient pattern and all the past pain I'd endured because of it. And I felt the connection between my conditioning as a child and the persona I carried on my back, a clear relationship between spinal problems and feeling unworthy. Channa was right. I was trying to secure a connection with the group so that inwardly I could feel love. The love I didn't feel was about me and had nothing to do with them.

The next day, I went back to Channa and thanked him for setting me free. Channa had helped me see something deep inside that I had no idea I'd been carrying for so long, and I humbly received his teaching. Because of this healing, I was able to enjoy more space in my body. I didn't need to compress my spine; I could walk tall in the freedom of who I am. There's beauty in the release of an old pattern, and less effort is required now for me to be who I was always meant to be. It was a true homecoming.

As I continue my spiritual growth, I realize that nothing on the outside can set me free, not even my teacher. He skillfully opened me up to look at and inquire about what I was doing and my conditioning, but ultimately it's me who has the responsibility and capability to set myself free.

Are You Ready to Teach?

During my second and third retreats in Bali with Channa, I was more open to whatever I experienced and less resistant to my own healing. By then, we had moved back to America, and six students from my classes in California came with me to the third retreat. Channa gave me more responsibilities: I was registrar, scheduled the massages, and also taught some of the classes. He never told me when I'd be teaching until the last minute, which was probably just as well, so I didn't have enough time to get anxious. Jumping into the unknown, in fact, became a great ride for me.

After one class, I went up to Channa's room where he was talking with the beautiful, pregnant Balinese girl who served us food daily. She was the one I mentioned earlier who was told she should not work, but stay in bed resting, as there were complications with her pregnancy. Channa had given her money, and he also gave her a healing, and she seemed thankful as she wiped away her tears in gratitude.

We had been served breakfast in the room, and I offered her my papaya juice. As I did, I could feel that Channa was not pleased with my actions. After the beautiful girl left, Channa asked if I could see that she was being taken care of, that all her needs had been met and that she was being held on all levels. "Yes," I said. "Why would you give her your juice, then?" he asked. I remember replying it was because I felt deeply for her and thought she would enjoy it. "To the outside world, this looks like I'm being tough on you, with such a kind act, but later you'll realize why this is an important lesson for you."

I was sad and angry, and began crying and telling him I was sorry. He said, "It's not about being sorry; it's about your own realizations. When you are in a similar situation at your center in America, you'll see why." I don't think he was criticizing my offering juice, but was emphasizing two things: first knowing your place in a particular situation. In that moment, the Balinese girl was already being taken care of and all I needed to do was be present and witness. Second, I see now how helpfulness can be a hindrance to knowing one's own needs and exercising *self*-care. Having a center of my own now and having the role of teacher, I sometimes see this in my students and think I understand it a bit more, although it's still a work in progress for me.

During my third Bali retreat, I came down with a bad cold on day two and had a fever and upper respiratory infection for the next three days. A nurse in our group offered me antibiotics. Normally I don't take them, but I could see this had taken a turn for the worse. I still came to class and served my teacher, but mostly I was on my back resting, experiencing some deep healing. I felt held on all levels, and lighter in a way, like who I'm not was leaving me and my soul was emerging through my heart's membrane as pure energy no longer hidden from consciousness.

Four days into the retreat, Channa got sick, too. He felt nauseous and vomited. It felt like an energy release. One night we were all massaging him and wiping the sweat from his forehead as we watched our teacher lay in pain, yet so sweetly at the same time. It felt to me that even though his body was going through something that none of us could explain, he was somehow removed from the suffering—experiencing it, yet not living from it.

We had three more days to go on the retreat, and he turned to me and said, "Mellara, are you ready to teach the rest of the retreat?' This wasn't something we'd ever talked about, and I replied, "No Channa, I'm not ready, but if you would like me to, I will. I'm here to support you in any way, and if that means teaching the rest of the retreat, I will." Channa replied, "If you teach tomorrow, my guides are saying the students will all walk out, as they are expecting me." I did end up teaching and no one walked out, I think because after Channa's comment that night, it gave me room to pause and reflect. I was beginning to realize that I just needed to be me in the room teaching. Seems simple enough. But the me I needed to be was the real and sometimes vulnerable me who was still undergoing healing.

As uncomfortable as it was for my ego, it was the only way. Just as Channa taught me in Australia to be a friend to my son Charlie, I needed to be that friend to myself and refrain from filling any big teaching role, but instead remain humble and present. I wasn't there playing a movie role as a teacher, nor was I there playing the role of Channa's mini-me. This was still confusing at the time because I was painfully rewiring the way I looked out and saw the world. My prospective was shifting, so the way I needed to teach and be in the world would also need to change. I knew that eventually I would need to have healed enough to where I was teaching from the scar and not the wound. This teaching journey was a journey in and of its self that didn't happen overnight; in fact, it took years. This retreat would be a pivotal pitstop in my growth where I would begin the process of calling back my power, simply by being me.

With Channa unwell it was giving all of us a taste of mortality and a lesson about how short life really is. Watching my teacher in pain, although I didn't feel he was dying, helped me to realize that someday we all die, including my beloved teacher. I guess I knew this intellectually but as it came into my body as an understanding I was saddened. I just wasn't ready for him to go just yet. But it did help me to see the importance of being present with the ones we love. Taking the time to say goodbye to them in the morning and letting them go with love to live their lives as they would like to. I do this pretty much every time I say goodbye to a loved one, friend, or student. I envision them healthy and happy as they walk away and send them my love. We just never know if that might be the last and final day we see them, and to not make this into something terribly sad, but in being aware of this we are celebrating them, our connection and the love we share.

Through experiences like these on retreat, I am coming to know more of my mind, heart, and body, and I acknowledge the grace that uplifts me, even when my body gets tired. I've promised myself that I'll continue to protect the light that has been kindled inside me and allowed me to heal so much. My gratitude and respect for life itself and love for all beings has deepened, and my heart has opened, allowing my abilities and virtues to grow. Now when I offer gratitude for the practice, I feel somehow protected. I was taken care of on such a deep level by my teacher and the Balinese staff, and I feel a calling to give back. The gifts I've received from them and others have helped me heal—to trust and realize that there is good in the world and I'm part of this good and can pay it forward. I also acknowledge the grace that has come into my life, and even if my mind becomes filled with dark thoughts and doubts, I'll remember my times in Bali and on retreat with Channa and in doing so, I can feel an unshakeable support.

CHAPTER FIFTEEN

Reverence

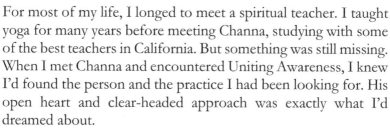

For most of my life, I longed to meet a spiritual teacher. I taught yoga for many years before meeting Channa, studying with some of the best teachers in California. But something was still missing. When I met Channa and encountered Uniting Awareness, I knew I'd found the person and the practice I had been looking for. His open heart and clear-headed approach was exactly what I'd dreamed about.

I feel I was guided to Channa. Our family moved to Australia, I believe, so I could be with him. As the blue sky meets the green grass, we are no different from the stars in the sky, and for those of us who are called, we can use this truth to change the world. My teacher represents for me the love that resides in the deepest place in my soul. He is the outer representation of the truth that resides within me, and in each of us. I pray all beings might feel this kind of devotion toward themselves and the representations of guidance they encounter within and without.

Having this time with Channa has opened me to depths in myself I was unable to reach before. I love being linked to a spiritual lineage; it's like drawing from the well of time. Spiritual paths can be like playing telephone—the essence of the message gets distorted over time. For millennia, we humans have fought each other to determine who has the one true God. After the Crusades, the Inquisition, the conquest of the Americas, World Wars I and II, civil wars far and wide including in my teacher's country, Sri Lanka, ethnic cleansing in Bosnia and Burma, and oh so many more genocides and holocausts, the result has been despair, carnage, and increased hatred.

Our task in the twenty-first century is to heal ourselves through conscious awareness. As we widen the circle of the knowable, we expand consciousness and extend our love. Living in awareness holds no sectarian allegiances and supports the faith of each individual, encouraging everyone to be aware of what is happening within and around them, moment after moment, and to dwell in the truth of that.

Trust

Eventually my husband came with me on a retreat to Bali, and it felt wonderful to have him there. It was a big deal to leave our kids at home and be so far away from them. But we trusted them and left them in good hands. We FaceTimed with them in the area where the wifi was strongest—it was so fun to connect with them in that way. We both missed them terribly, but it also felt right that we were together on a healing retreat and in such an exquisite part of the world.

My love for my teacher was strong and with Bali as the backdrop, my husband by my side, and the sun's rays so sweetly on my face, it awakened me many times to the direct connection that I have to my true nature and to others. This was the awakening to Self I'd yearned for, the bliss in the hearing of a distant bird chirping, the essence inside all that we are one.

The more I feel the power of this devotion and the blessings that come from my commitment to a teacher and a practice, the more innocent and humble I feel. The more a spiritual teacher feels the student's devotion, I've read, the freer they are to take on everything for you, holding gently the sufferings, delusions, and other dark traits that aren't actually yours. This practice helps me see the arising of ego, and in witnessing I'm able to create the space for a life worth living, and to stop generating the obstacles that tangle me.

Because I trust in my teacher and have faith that he's guiding me well, devotion is simple and has led to a sweet surrender. The devotion I feel is not blind, nor is it relinquishing my freedom or the responsibilities I have to myself and my family, despite how it might have looked to others at the time. My primary devotion was to healing myself, because I knew from deep within that if I could heal myself, I would become a better human being, mother, daughter, sister, friend, and wife. This practice consistently points its way toward healing and a deeper connection to Self. In its purest form, my devotion to my teacher and the practice is commensurate to the respect and love I have for my own higher space and personal growth. This trust continues to build in me, and I'm now blessed with the opportunity to share these teachings.

To watch Channa's devotion to his teachers is an inspiration for me. His Buddhist upbringing and the guidance of his mother, grandmother, and the elderly monk he studied with in Sri Lanka were probably his main teachers. Another important teacher was Sivakami Sonia Sumar, a Brazilian yoga teacher. Sonia began teaching yoga for children with special needs in the early 1970s, when her daughter was born with Down syndrome and she discovered that yoga was helpful. She studied the teachings of Sri Swami Sivananda in Brazil, and later opened a center near Chicago under the auspices of Swami Satchidananda. Her book *Yoga for the Special Child* has been published in four languages, and she continues to conduct workshops and training programs throughout the world.

Sonia came into Channa's life after he already had opened the Dassanayaka Yoga Centre. A parent who had a child with special needs asked whether Channa could assist them. He tried some intuitive techniques successfully, and then he heard Sonia Sumar was teaching in Sydney. So he flew there to attend her course, and when he met her, he says he felt profoundly connected to her energetically. After that class, he flew to the US to attend a course at her center near Chicago, and after that, he went to Brazil to study with her some more. When he finished his teacher training, he returned to Australia and taught special needs children from newborns to twelve-year-olds. The lesson, he says, is that "in a nutshell, we're all special needs."

Later, Sonia Sumar came to Melbourne twice, to visit and to teach. It was a great opportunity for Channa to look after his teacher. "I cooked for her and for all the workshop participants. I was busy but she insisted I also attend the class." During her first visit, she performed a beautiful ceremony and blessed the center including the backyard. Later, we transformed the yard into a beautiful garden with living quarters for Darren and Channa, and when she visited the second time, she stayed in the house.

"The presence of Sonia Sumar was very important for me," Channa told me. "It was a milestone on my path and a formation for my journey, affirming that I was on the right path. She has lived a life of service and has a lot of wisdom. It's beautiful to be around her and learn the importance of life and service."

Experiencing Truth

While at a breakfast gathering one day, Channa talked to us about truth. He said truth is more a feeling than a knowing, something we can experience through our breath, heart, and body.

A new student asked, "Sometimes it's hard to understand this practice. I go home and google some of the things you talk about, but I'm still searching." Channa replied, "Over time you'll see who you are. You'll see the places you get stuck, and through authentic inquiry, you'll come to understand more clearly. When you feel tired, why are you tired? Tired of what? Maybe tired of all the BS. The word *God* is not God. The word *food* is not food. One day, you'll realize that words cannot satiate you or give you life, or peace. They separate. Even the philosophy I'm describing is ultimately not satisfying. *Surrender*, for example, is not just a word. It's a realization. Philosophies are important, but their promises are empty. Philosophies rarely help anyone realize the truth. Truth is beyond words.

"When we're on retreat in Bali, we study the lotus. It doesn't mean we open up the computer and study scientific research about lotuses. We go to the garden and sit with the lotus flower. We feel it, observe, see it in sunlight, see it in moonlight, feel it with the rain, feel it in the breeze, and see it in each moment. This is different from sitting in a library researching online." Channa is well-versed in psychology, religious studies, and Eastern wisdom, a one-stop shop of conscious truth education, and he shares these teachings with many. But he always considers knowledge, his and others', to be secondary to *experience*.

Devotion to the truth comes naturally to me. Studying with Channa, the further I dove into consciousness and could see truth, I felt the need to understand more. Sometimes I would pinch myself in class, as I felt I was experiencing an awakened being right before my eyes. But then attachment arises, and I have to witness it. Listening to the teachings, envisioning the possibility of a transformative experience, thoughts arise from a place of ambition and desire. I witness it, without adding more.

The Path of Devotion

The path of devotion is the road less travelled in the West, and many spiritual swindlers have reinforced the negative side of this path. There is no verification process of competency, or pathways that ensure authenticity. But the time is now to awaken from greed and the glorification of ego, and stop being ignorant of the truth of who we really are. My children sometimes say to me, "But Mom, other kids are doing it, why can't we?" and my response is always, "Just because they have it or do it doesn't mean it's right for you."

From the time I met Channa, I never wanted to be away from him. When he would speak, I hear truth in nearly every word. It was like a pin dropping and we all could hear it, because truth resonates with a silent observer within. But we have to check the truth we receive from others against our own deep inner knowing. We don't so much *receive* truth from others as we *respond* to truth with the tuning fork of our own intuition.

With so much disharmony and hatred in the world today, it's ever so important that we learn discernment. This will protect us and ensure our self-preservation, because the world is engaged in a cycle of power-hungry leadership, a creation of our own making. A dear friend I've known since I was twelve was concerned about me, fearing I was deferring too much to Channa. She felt I didn't realize my own value as a teacher and was negating almost twenty years of teaching yoga and giving short shrift to my previous teachers. She thought I was turning into a Channa wannabe, a kind of clone. But this *is* the real me, uncovered after a lifetime of persona-producing. Honoring my teacher is not separate from honoring the light in me—and in all beings. Of course, sometimes, perhaps often, that which my friend was concerned about was true. Many followers take on characteristics of their teachers, confusing truth with mimicking others. We always have to ask ourselves, "What is true?" and explore all aspects deeply. It's rarely if ever 100 percent this, or 100 percent that. "In every joke, there is a little truth," people say. In Russia, someone often adds, "In every joke, there is a little joke."

But my ego was hurt when my friend and Mike, who shared her concern, were talking behind my back. I lashed out at them, and later asked for their forgiveness. I forgave myself too. They had raised real questions, and even if they were misperceiving, I had to honor their perspective and their love for me, while still honoring my own truth and knowing what my soul needed in the moment for its own healing.

At the end of the day, they were just being protective of me and were unsure about Channa's motives or trustworthiness. There have been so many bad apples among spiritual teachers, and their fears were grounded in that reality. They were not experiencing what I was on a daily basis, and if for a time I looked like a Sri Lankan wannabe—something even my son noticed and teased me about—I was learning something important from my teacher. Now I know that the biggest compliment we can give any teacher is to not to *be* them but to learn *from* them, allowing the *essence* of their generosity and teachings to flow through us as we become more whole and wholly ourselves.

Looking Deeply

It was painful for my ego not to get my husband and my dear friend's approval. I wanted them to understand my perspective, and for that I suffered. It has taken a while for me to realize I don't need to convince anyone of anything. It's for them to experience for themselves, even when their reality is different from mine. As I've come to feel more settled in myself and what I care about, others have been able to open to my experience.

Over time, I've also come to see my part. I have many dependency issues that showed up in my relationship with an older man when I was fifteen and two marriages before Mike—always on the lookout for someone (or something) to provide the support and admiration I hadn't been able to give myself. I've looked for men to take care of me, because I didn't feel worthy or "enough." The origins of this tendency are deep, and slowly I'm starting to understand its hold on me. It's been a "thing" all my life, and I'm now able to acknowledge that being with my teacher, although it includes many beautiful, unconditioned qualities, also includes elements of my need for the love and approval of a parent-figure.

Sometimes, of course, it's reasonable to depend on others. As children we depend on our parents to meet our needs during many stages of growing up, and when our needs are met, we don't go through life looking for Mr. Good Father and Ms. Good Mother. I try my best to meet my kids in a way that shows them how deeply loved and supported they are, and now as they're getting older, it's amazing to see the many ways I'm becoming redundant! They're making their own lunches, their own beds, and getting their homework done because they want to. I try to keep a conscious eye on them, realizing when they need support and encouragement, yet not helicoptering over them.

Being with my teacher, as I look back, has included dependence. I've wanted his approval, and so I did things to please him, like staying longer at the center in Melbourne even when it cut into the travel time I needed to pick up the kids at school. And then returning to the States, I took his phone calls even when it wasn't the best time for my family. A lot of our phone conversations were about logistical details of retreats and building our new centers, but he would also give me a personal teaching, knowing in granular detail what was happening in my life, and I came to yearn for his calls, desperately seeking reparenting. Only now am I able to own that dimension of my relationship with Channa.

Although my dependence on my teacher wasn't obvious to me, it was to others. Another dear friend told me, "I don't have issues with Channa, I have issues with you devoting your whole life to him. You even sound like him when you're teaching." It was something that I was slowly working on and she was right. Like a child star does, it was almost like I was growing up in front of everyone and it was really painful at times. I guess now as I look back without feeling defensive, I believe Channa was hoping I'd see this for myself, but he never said anything straight out. That's usually how he worked with us. I think we need to be ready to hear something before we can let it in. Realizations are deepest when they come from us and our inner world.

I've continued looking for the security and encouragement that a child needs well into adulthood, and especially with Channa. It's a slippery slope. Just as the birds are dependent on the sky, the student is dependent on the teacher, and the teacher the student. We support each other. But there are healthy boundaries, and I'm still learning about this every day, looking to see if some action or thought is causing harm to myself or others. As a more mature relationship with myself unfolds, a more mature relationship with my teacher does also, calling forth mutual respect. Each moment I look inside to see if I'm staying true to myself.

A genuine teacher won't demand that you give up everything you know to be true, yet there were moments I thought I needed to do just that. I was unable to distinguish between reverence and self-abandonment. I'm pretty sure Channa saw this too, because one day in our kitchen in California, he told Mike and me, "Mellara needs to be with her family more." I remember feeling angry, because I was with my family a lot and also with my teacher. Perhaps this was a wake-up call.

I was so devoted to Channa, it was hard to find a balance with my life's other loves and responsibilities. We can't just live for others. I'm still sitting with these hard questions and see boundary-making as a way of respecting both myself and others. In addition to my family, my yoga teaching, and Channa, I have a responsibility to care for my body, which is on loan, and my thoughts and emotions that arrive at my doorstep seeking attention. Today I'm causing less suffering for myself and others as I continue to grow and develop. I'm less involved with my stories, and the stories of others. There's more calm and composure in my life as I don't require quite as much approval from my teacher, my husband, and my kids.

I believe Channa never wanted me to be anything more or less than who I am. He always mirrors my own nature in ways that are like a river flowing. What I do know for certain is that creating a life where I suffer less is my priority. Perhaps a certain amount of dependence, independence, codependence, and interdependence along the path of healing are needed and in some ways unavoidable. If a student has experienced trauma in their life—and if they haven't it isn't likely they will embark on a path of healing and deeper understanding— they probably need nurturing and then a connection to an awakened being, experiencing a field of unconditioned love. Touching the space of a human heart is the most magical and healing sensation for both parties.

We evolve, and when we do we're never the same again. We can't return to the so-called bliss of ignorance or the complacency of avoidance. We come to a healing practice with a jagged autobiography. Things don't make sense, and we can't wrap our heads around the dramas, traumas, joys, losses, and chapters of our lives that move too quickly to find our breath. Or perhaps we come to the practice because we're not feeling quite right, or we've gotten too involved in something or it's hard to move through the pain. All these things disturb the flow of our lives, and we will pay a high price to regain our balance, to stay in homeostasis. Going on retreat or having a practice is a way to move into acceptance and it's not always blissful. We are trying to enter into a relationship with all the pieces of ourselves, not just the sweet parts we like, but the rejected bitter parts as well. And we try to do it with wisdom and compassion.

Channa is a true spiritual teacher. He is kind, humble, and compassionate, and he never gave up on me when I tried to make him into the mother and the father I never had. He held that space for me as I worked hard to allow in the painful truth of the self I project and my real being. Channa holds space for all, and turns no one away. The truth of his words and his follow-through have kept me on the path of truth-seeking and devotion. Buddha-nature, the capacity of awakening, is in all of us, and when it comes alive inside, the blessings and power of the practice transform all beings.

CHAPTER SIXTEEN

Returning Home

Just as Channa had said the first time I met him, in less than two years after arriving in Melbourne, we were back living in California. Although I felt a strong desire to stay in Australia longer, I knew that if I focused on the practice, I could live anywhere. Because of these magnificent teachings and an unwavering devotion to my teacher as a representation of the care I now have for my own inner work, my true home is wherever I'm living fully present. I made a vow of sorts to be married to the practice.

Leela seemed excited to be back home in her bedroom that she had known since being a curious toddler right around the time when Charlie was born. Charlie who is basketball crazy began to connect the dots of being able to watch American college and NBA games in real time. So that made him very happy! Just like Leela he walked right into his old bedroom, the only one he has known other than sharing one in Australia with Leela. Mike seemed happy too as our home in the Bay Area is spacious and roughly half the monthly cost of the small townhome we rented in Melbourne. Mike cares about finances and that, along with his deep affinity and love for San Francisco, led to him feeling like we made the right decision for our family at the time.

Returning to the US in 2015, the politics had changed. Donald Trump was one of seventeen candidates for the Republican presidential nomination. I remember seeing Channa before we left and making a joke about it. Channa turned around and said, "This is where the world is headed. He will be your next president." I laughed, but Channa didn't. He had a serious look on his face. When I told Mike, he laughed too, and said that Americans would never let that happen.

Once home in my garden in California I realized that I was inside a new chapter of my life and, even though I was happy about it, the reality begin to sink in. One lone tear fell from my eye and a few more after that. Even though I'd done everything possible to spend as much time as I could with Channa while we were in Melbourne, it didn't feel like enough. Yet it was also an exciting new beginning and a chance for me to spread my wings with all I'd learned. Being able to share Channa's teachings is my joy and honor, and he was encouraging me to take flight. The moment and the task required me to move beyond doubts and fears. I just needed to be a good tool in the shed, and to honor the grace Channa had bestowed onto me. I vowed to be a steward of the practice, always learning, listening for inner guidance, and cultivating the trust that is the ground of the devotion I feel for my teacher. It was also a high priority for me to get Channa to come to the US to teach. Channa had not taught in the US before but seemed ready and suggested it—he had been talking about it for quite a while when we were in Australia. When I told him that we were moving back to America he didn't seemed fazed. It seemed like he had already seen it play out in his mind.

Although we went through all the known hassles of an international move, this time our belongings arrived in just under six weeks. And now I had the support of a teacher and felt ready for all that life might bring my way. Mike and the children carried their own weight through the transition, and they lifted me up with them. I felt the space to breathe deeply into all that is me. I am the old oak tree in the yard that holds the wisdom of the ages, and I am my children for whom I care so deeply. Even though we had moved to the other side of the planet, again, I could feel my beloved teacher in the grace of the hummingbirds and the wind chimes outside our door. I knew my life was now worth living and, as my teacher says, we've gathered here on earth to become one with life.

The Stream of Life

One day early on during my stay in Melbourne, Channa told our class, "If the cosmos has a rhythm, we're all in that rhythm; if the cosmos has a flow, we're all in that flow. We can choose to swim against it. We can choose to leave the flow and move to the river rock along the way. But the river continues, and we're free to enjoy the ride."

In the course of our move back to the US, I began to feel a connection with the unknown. I noticed how the *knowns* in my life were of much more concern than the *unknowns*. What I don't know doesn't have the power to hurt me, and what I do know I can create stories around, so I made note to be aware of that. Flowing with the river of life as it is opens us to the magic in each moment. And if within our moments we are trying to present an image that isn't who we are, life can feel unsettling.

I generally feel more anchored to my truest self when I am in the stream of not-knowing. Not-knowing has nothing to do with intelligence or not planning things—it is an energetic choice to live life more freely and with less stress. We can be quite versed on many subjects yet simultaneously live from a place of not knowing. We can let go of controlling our outer life because we are much more trusting in our inner life as it naturally unfolds. But we are not generally taught to like the unknowns of life. Living in awareness, even when things appear from seemingly nowhere, means caring for ourselves in the highest vibrational way, flowing with what we are given and to not making it into something that it isn't. We just allow the moment to be, rather than swimming against it, or trying to change it, or making it disappear.

By being the observer, we can be awed and astounded by just how interesting our life is from this advantage point.

Living in awareness is vast, and yet it is not separate from the smallest of details of our life. Every day I'm learning to embody compassion and serve more deeply. Until returning to the States, I didn't have the courage to move beyond the knowns. Now I trust the guidance that I feel within. Making an effort to know my neighbors, for example, has become an important practice for me. It's a way of saying "yes" to life, not building walls to fortify myself in order to feel safe and unchallenged.

Once we returned home, we were in a whirlwind of events: catching up with friends we hadn't seen in a long time, getting back into our house, and remembering how things are done in the States. In just two years, the valleys east of the Berkeley Hills had become much more crowded, and even driving locally was sometimes stressful. But with the practice within me, I could face each new day like savoring a piece of apple pie with ice cream.

Before returning, we gave our tenants three months' notice so they could find another place, and in barely more than a month they'd moved out. That gave us plenty of time to begin replacing old windows and making improvements to the kitchen that hadn't been altered since the house was built sixty years before. The work ended up taking six months, so our first months at home we were living in a construction zone—washing dishes in the bathtub, then cleaning the tub and getting the kids ready for bed was a lot. We did our best, using the outdoor grill and the microwave, or eating out.

I also wanted to build the studio in the backyard sooner rather than later, but Mike wasn't on board, saying I could teach in the house and students could use the kids' bathroom. I was not up for that. We had several conversations about the studio and slowly Mike understood that I wasn't going to give up on the idea. After a few months of talking about it, he finally wrapped his head around it and started to help me with the planning of it.

While in Australia, I never spent more than five minutes on the phone with Channa. I was in his classes daily, and he always reminded us, "I'm not your phone or texting buddy, I'm your teacher." But when we returned to California, he began calling frequently. He always seemed to know when to call, reaching out within minutes when there was something uneasy inside me. It was unexpected and felt wonderful. He would give me a teaching, ask about my day, and then I would carry on. At the same time, he was going through his own transition. His landlord on Bastings Street had just passed away. On his deathbed, the land-lord assured Channa he could continue to rent the house at the same rate, but the landlord's son refused to honor his father's wish and raised the rent significantly. After seventeen years living and teaching yoga there, Channa had to move. He handled it all with aplomb, but I felt tense, wanting to help.

The children were back at the school they were familiar with (with classes in English!), and we gave Leela the puppy she'd always dreamed of. Everything seemed well on the outside, but inside something was getting the best of me.

A New Day

Once Mike, Leela, Charlie, and I settled into our routines and our life back in California stabilized, it was easier for me to feel how much I was still changing—continuing to shed layers of who I'm not. My inner growth was still very much in motion. This was not going to be a rerun of my life before moving Down Under.

Before we left Australia, Channa warned me that my friends would be looking for the person they knew before I moved. I didn't understand what he meant, but as I began meeting up with old friends, they weren't at all interested in who I had become or even what I'd been doing. I tried meeting them where they were in the hopes of pleasing them and easing the tension, but it didn't work. I couldn't support their stories or my own old fabrications anymore. Some old friendships were drifting away.

One day on the phone Channa advised me, "Help them evolve, Mellara, don't get drawn in." By not supporting their stories about me, I was choosing freedom and manifesting a life where blame, shame, and insecurities could be felt deeply without being acted upon. Like my friend in Australia, they did not approve of Channa even though they had never met him. I was headstrong about it and felt like Channa and his teachings were good for me, whereas my girlfriends were worried that it was all too much, too soon. It wasn't easy, as friends seemed to feel threatened by this change, and some wrote harsh emails while others chose silence. I knew it wasn't their fault that I had changed. And I knew it wasn't for me to convince them of anything. I was discovering a freedom within that I'd never known before. I wasn't tethered to the cord of destruction. My interests were changing, yet I looked the same and that was hard for them.

Perhaps this kind of growth is inevitably confrontative. If my friends wanted to continue together, we couldn't just relive the old ways. One friend who was originally my student wanted to help me get Channa's message out while at the same time she saw me as his equal doing my own teachings separate from Channa. She had been in music management for years and knew all too well the pitfalls of having business partnerships and the mess it creates when the honeymoon is over. She was looking out for me like a dear sister, but I wasn't having it—to me she was wrong about Channa. She was trying to warn me against it, but at the same time she saw the value of us working alongside each other. She had experienced this before with musicians she had worked with in the past who had Indian gurus. She was skeptical about Channa and his intentions.

I was beginning to understand where she was coming from until I got a phone call from Channa. He seemed quite upset with me that I would even consider that my friend was correct. We just left it there, and my friend and I didn't speak again after that which was very sad. I could tell that Mike also felt that there was some truth and sound advice coming from my friend, and that drove a wedge between Mike and me for some time. But Mike also reminded me of what he said after his day-long retreat with Channa when we first moved to Australia. He said that he could see why Channa liked being around me as a teacher because I had a lot that I could offer him too. I asked him what he meant when he said this and he said that my teaching of the asanas and the general way that I taught yoga was complementary to the way Channa teaches, and that we could possibility help each other. Mike believes in me and especially as a teacher, he always has—after all this was the way we met each other.

But it was still really hard to take in Mike and my friends' concerns about me and my relationship with Channa, I think primarily because I thought I had found a sense of belonging with Channa and his world and I didn't want anyone to take that away from me. This was the little Mellara speaking, the one who didn't get her needs met as a child and was yearning and fighting to keep that kind of love and belonging I finally found with Channa. It was a really difficult time.

During this time, my relationship with the natural world was blossoming. When we returned to California, it was summertime, and after Mike and the kids settled in for the night, I would lie down in our backyard for hours, listening to the sounds of crickets. I never did that before. I felt so much more connected to my surroundings, living and tasting each moment. Just a few days after we returned home, I was walking in the backyard envisioning where the yoga studio might go, and Channa called, saying his guides told him there were lots of bees buzzing in my garden. I couldn't believe it, because in that moment, hundreds of bees were enjoying the plethora of lavender plants right in front of me.

Our whole family was going through a period of growth, and I witnessed the field of practice transform all of us. If one person in a family is living in awareness, the effects ripple widely. Channa teaches through the way he lives, and he lets people in. If they stay, leave, or come back, he is filled with compassion toward them. I've watched many people return to Channa's circle of friends and students after leaving, including some who had caused him problems, and I saw the depth of forgiveness he offers. Channa told me he never forgets what happens to him, but he also offers the energy of forgiveness. "It's a completely new day," he said.

Returning to America, I had to let go of what *was* in order to be true to myself. In the past I would withdraw from uncomfortable situations, or protect myself with boundaries, out of fear of being myself. I was unable to see that who I really am is with me in all I do, including when I contract and run away. Realizing this, I began to feel lighter, no longer bearing the weight of the world on my shoulders. At the end of the day, just doing my best is enough. This "best" is often filled up with mistakes, my ego rearing its ugly head. What's different is that I'm catching it sooner and witnessing. Humility helps. I learned this by watching my teacher.

Now I dwell in the unknown with a joy that can't be explained. I simply allow things to unfold, whether good or bad—it doesn't matter, it's all a dance, what Sanskrit calls *leela*, or divine play. I celebrate my sense of *being*. I no longer identify with my ideas, actions, roles, or ambitions. Even my fear of death has been replaced by awe and wonder for each day. I'm a fish swimming in sacred sensations, living my fullest life one moment at a time.

CHAPTER SEVENTEEN

Only Change Remains the Same

A woman who was unable to get pregnant, even after in vitro fertilization, was referred to Channa for a healing. He said that her energy needed to be cleared, that souls come down when they're ready, and he worked with her for weeks. Finally she gave birth to a beautiful baby boy, and she wrote Channa a heartfelt letter of thanks. She showed the letter to a friend, the former yoga student who had referred her to Channa for healing. When the friend learned that the Dassayanaka Yoga Centre had to move from Bastings Street due to a steep rent increase, she told her dad, who owned a fixer-upper nearby. So her dad offered the property to Dassanayaka Yoga at a modest rent. Channa saw the potential and encouraged us to work together to make this building our new home.

Channa and Darren held community meetings and reviewed proposals, offers, and opportunities. As discussions boiled down to decisions, Channa signed the lease and construction began for a new yoga and healing center. Channa sees yoga teachers taking care of the spirit in the way doctors and nurses take care of their patients' physical needs. His plans for the center included a studio for yoga and meditation and rooms for Ayurveda, naturopathy, and massage. The space would be community-based, with new teachers and practitioners coming on board to help the center grow. Eventually, there would be living quarters in the backyard for Channa.

Even while closing up the Bastings Street center and preparing to rebuild the fixer-upper, Channa continued giving classes and helping students through difficulties. One week he helped a couple through separation and freed the spirit of a grandmother who was haunting the family home. On one of our phone calls, when I questioned all the things going on in his life, he said we have to find a balance on all levels and asked, "Would you wait to feed Charlie until Leela is finished? No, you give them food at the same time. It's important to take care of the community when it's needed, not by my preferred timeline."

Along with the yoga community raising funds for the new center, Channa spent three years working on projects and taking part in fundraising events around the world to help this happen. The first donation came from Channa himself; he sold family heirlooms and personal items from his childhood home to launch the fundraising campaign. Fundraising goals were met in 2020, and Dassanayaka Yoga Australia reopened as Uniting Awareness in the summer of 2020.

Being Present

Watching Channa deal so gracefully with change and flux taught me again the importance of being present, something I had learned back in the early days at Dassanayaka Yoga in Melbourne, when I was new to the practice. Channa had asked me to do something for him. I was new to the center and excited to do it. I was already feeling such a deep connection. So I hastily agreed, and while walking backwards away from him and nodding my head eagerly, I accidentally walked right into his beloved mother's elephant shrine. When I turned to see what I'd walked into, I knocked the tiny door on his shrine where the candles are stored and hurt myself a little as well. Fortunately the shrine and the door were okay, but my ego was a little bruised.

Channa called me back and asked if I was okay, then added, "Mellara, please slow down enough to feel your steps." Hearing his words and taking a deep breath, I knew that my practice and healing were very much an ongoing process, probably for this whole lifetime. So I placed my palms together in prayer and bowed my head, walking out with every ounce of my beingness connecting with my body, every step taken with care and attention.

I came to see that a lot of my suffering is brought on by my own reactivity, separating myself from my family and from the world. Responding to life rather than reacting to it has become my new mantra. As a child, I covered my being quite well and identified with pains, untruths, and conditioning. The being or spirit in me is now my priority. I see myself as a spirit having a human experience and with this understanding I now slow down enough to feel my life as worthy.

California Dream

Just as Channa was building a new yoga center in Melbourne, Mike and I were exploring ways to construct Dassanayaka Yoga in our Bay Area, California, backyard. Mike and I began reconnecting again after a loving kindness workshop, and we made the effort to be with one another alone as a couple. He could see that my heart was in the right place, and that I wasn't trying to build a life outside of the one we shared.

We purchased a beautiful prefab house, and I was able to get the permits in just two days. We had heard horror stories about how long that process can take, so I just stayed in the building department and patiently witnessed the process, learning everyone's names in the office and bringing them coffee and treats during breaks. I had fun and felt real satisfaction doing this. The energy of my teacher and the practice was shining through me, and with each action I felt the miracle of living in awareness.

While building the studio in our backyard, I was also teaching in studios around town on Sundays. It wasn't easy at first, as I was offering a style of yoga people weren't familiar with. The practice I offered was gentle and had a deep spiritual component to it, while also weaving in yoga positions to breathe into. The classes that were generally offered back then in our area were more focused on the body's physical form. There is value in both styles of yoga, because as we embody the physical form it is our gateway into the soul. My style was bridging the two.

My classes were also different because from Channa, I had learned the value of not always having a plan for classes and relying on "reading the room" to discern what theme might be best given, depending upon what the primary energy feels like as students begin to arrive. The class becomes responsive to what the students are needing in that moment. I also didn't dress like other yoga folks and would often just wear a t-shirt or long sleeve peasant top and tights and not the usual trendy Lululemon garb. I wasn't trying to make a statement, it was simply that I had just come from Australia and there was less focus on what we wore to yoga class.

It was healing for me to teach; I was finding my voice and making sense of all I was going through. Because of this experience, I felt I could help others heal too. Teaching back-to-back classes took more out of me than it had before. I was tired in a different way. Each time I returned home, I craved green juices and lots of food. But I couldn't wait for Sundays so I could teach. It was like being in a holding pattern the rest of the week. One day Channa called and said everything I do is a class—talking with my children, stacking the dishwasher, folding laundry, or sipping tea. "Be with yourself, Mellara, and be with your students when you're teaching, without separation."

The first Dassanayaka Yoga retreat in California was in March 2017. I was thrilled to introduce Channa to forty-five of my students, who joined us for a three-day retreat in Sonoma. So many of the participants were profoundly helped by learning about living in awareness, yoga, and meditation, and absorbing the healing powers of nature.

Suzy Dito, who ten years ago was the woman who gave me my first yoga teaching job in San Francisco, was instrumental in organizing the retreat and Channa's visit to the US. By then, she was the membership and wellness director for the Presidio YMCA, where I first met her and taught. Without her, I'm not sure it would have happened. I'd never organized or led a retreat before, and we were both learning as we went. She was already a great yoga teacher, a dear friend, and someone I knew immediately that I could trust.

Suzy gave me a baby shower for Charlie in 2009, when I hadn't known her for that long. She helped Mike and me rent out our San Francisco apartment while we were in Australia. As an energy exchange, I offered to pay for half her trip to Bali to join me as I attended my second retreat with Channa there, and she jumped at the chance. Channa usually assigns each person a single room in Bali, but Suzy and I shared a room as she didn't know the others and Channa didn't want her to feel isolated.

At the beginning of the retreat, Channa gave each person a healing. When it was Suzy's turn, he took her outside and (no kidding!) thunder and lightning came. Chills went up and down my spine. After the ceremony, there was a light rain, but no more thunder and lighting. Afterward Suzy told me her life was changed profoundly by the retreat (and not just the healing and the clouds bursting open). From the moment we met, we both felt that we would do something together in the future, and today we often teach together in the Bay Area, leading daylong and longer retreats.

Mike and I offered Channa our bedroom to stay in before the Sonoma retreat, but he declined, saying he didn't want to disturb the energy of our home. "Mellara, don't you have an old shed in the backyard?" he asked. I said yes, but told him it's our storage garage. He said, "If you make it ready for me next time, I'll stay there." So he stayed with Suzy and her dog Siddhartha in San Francisco. I was sad, having hoped he would stay with us, but I trusted his decision. So along with making sure my kids got to school and had babysitters, I commuted to San Francisco every day to help host Channa's visit.

Westerbeke

The retreat was held at the deeply peaceful Westerbeke Ranch. We began by walking slowly, in procession, up the hill to the round room at the top of the property. Before entering the room, we washed our feet using a ladle of water that Suzy and I offered each person. Channa has us perform this ritual at the beginning of all his retreats. Then we each lit a candle and an incense stick, offered the incense in a large bowl just outside the door, and entered the room holding our candles. As we entered the room, we were greeted by hauntingly beautiful music* and an abundance of roses from our garden at home. The shrine was decorated with images of Buddha, Jesus, Mother Mary, and other deities, and the fragrant incense smoke, drifting in through the door, which was left ajar, added to the mystery. Then Channa blessed us, one by one, chanting in Pali. There was a profound feeling of acceptance, of everyone feeling seen and being worthy.

Channa's energy is healing just to be around, and during the opening of the retreat as he often does, he performed a healing ceremony with each individual. He gave each student his full attention, and each "healing" was unique. It was more than just one person healing and blessing us—together we were the co-creators of our healing. I had a feeling that most had never experienced anything like it. While waiting our turn, we were "held" by the fragrance of roses, the wafting of incense, and the shimmering of little tea lights. As our sense of joy and openness was building, Channa's body language and demeanor seemed serious and at the same time filled with love and compassion. After each individual healing, Channa placed that student's candle on the shrine while the rest of the group chanted OM, invoking a deeply uplifting energy.

The yoga sessions were varied and wonderful, never planned

---

* Craig Pruess and Ananda, "Devi Prayer," from *108 Sacred Names of Mother Divine* (Gloucestershire, UK: Heaven on Earth Music, 2002) https://www.youtube.com/watch?v=ic_pVkcLh9M. There was other music too, but this is the one that will remain in my heart forever.

as far as I could tell, and included meditation and insightful discussions led by Channa. Some meals were taken in meditative silence to fully appreciate the food, its source, and those who prepared it. The students all contributed to the care of the space by sweeping floors, cleaning the altar, and simply taking care of our own yoga mats and the space around us.

The message throughout the retreat was that we have the power to heal ourselves but it's usually hidden beneath layers of our own creation, often from early in life when we had to protect ourselves from the pain of not being seen for who we are. Channa touched on many subjects, including staying present with life's unknowns and somatic experiencing (being in the body without identifying with it). When fear, self-criticism, or anxiety arose, Channa encouraged us to invite it in and witness it, without letting it take us over.

During one class, Suzy and I both felt the presence of Paramahansa Yogananda, the great twentieth-century yogi, and Channa even began to sound like recordings of him we'd heard. It was as though Yogananda came through Channa to awaken us to our spiritual truths. Later, I learned that Yogananda had visited Luther Burbank, who was his student, not far from Westerbeke in the 1920s.[*]

Every evening after Darren brought Channa his dinner, Suzy and I went to his room where we found him in a lot of pain. His body was taking in a lot of the toxic energy the students were discharging, and we massaged him to bring his body back to life.

During this retreat, I started to develop a stronger personal practice. I began waking up naturally at 3:30 or 4:00 in the morning and meditated while listening to recordings of some of Channa's classes, which included guided meditations, yoga instruction, and teachings. After that, I'd write. Retreatants came to understand the importance of being mindful of everything—within and without—dwelling deeply in each moment. One student said, "Channa is a truly gifted individual who has a natural

---

[*] See Paramahansa Yogananda, *Autobiography of a Yogi* (Encinitas, California: Self-Realization Fellowship, 1994), 349-353.

ability to bring people together, to inspire and heal in a way I haven't witnessed before. Words can't fully describe the depth of this experience. My spirit has been touched forever."

Near the end of the retreat, we were sitting in a circle going around the room and checking in. A woman named India looked like she'd been going through a lot—things often come up in retreats—and she told us she hadn't slept well the night before. Out of the blue, Channa said to her, "There's someone next to you and she wants to tell you that she loves you and that she's alright." India burst into tears and said, "I know. That's my sister." She told us that her sister had been murdered when she was a teenager. "Because our whole family was upset with the choices she'd made, we didn't even give her a proper burial. I will forever feel grief and guilt about it." By now, India was crying uncontrollably, and on the spot, Channa asked if he could give her sister a Buddhist burial, and she said yes. He asked me to get a bowl and a jug of pure water, and asked the group to sit closer together in the circle. We began chanting OM while Channa chanted in Pali and began pouring the water slowly into the bowl. Time stood still, and I swear more water came out of that jug than I'd put in it! This beautiful student was grateful and visibly shaken. I'm sure she never expected anything like that to happen in her lifetime.

Suzy and I were blown away by this and so many of the experiences during the retreat. We were really pleased that forty-five students had come and were able to experience Channa's presence directly. We'd only planned for twenty, but people kept signing up. Many left with a clarity of mind they hadn't felt for a long time.

Mike was with us too on retreat and something happened to him that weekend; he became softer, more open, and his feminine nurturing, caring, relating energy was renewed. I love this energy in Mike and could feel his open heart—it felt so good to be with him. In my opinion, our world needs a deeper connection to the feminine energy and to let go of the "power-over" aggressive patriarchal model of leadership. The nurturing energy of the Mother, including Mother Earth, has been lost. On the macrocosm, rebalancing masculine and feminine energy will help us heal as a planet, but on the microcosm, it has had a noticeable impact on our family. Months after Channa left, my children continued to feel the benefits of both their parents being more balanced.

Soft Opening

Channa returned that fall, and the first opening of the yoga studio in our yard was on October 19, 2017.* Channa performed a puja ceremony. Mike and the kids were involved too, and it felt very auspicious, like a wedding. Channa hadn't known October 19 was my birthday; he selected the date because of the new moon, and it felt like a real gift, a new beginning, a new life, a new day. Twenty-five or thirty people came. With Channa as chef de cuisine, we all helped make spinach with dal from his cookbook *Sri Lankan Flavours,* and yellow rice, his mom's favorite. He called it "God's rice." Now, every new moon, I teach at the backyard studio and prepare these two dishes. The studio opened for classes in January 2018. Once the Covid-19 pandemic entered our lives in March of 2020, I had to take my classes online, like most yoga teachers. I still teach on the new moon but now the students cook their own lentils and rice at home while we find our way through this new normal.

Before meeting Channa, I would complain about my roles in life—daughter, mother, sister, wife. I did this because I hadn't experienced the rest of me, the still, quiet, imperturbable place where I'm now able to take refuge when my external world is disturbed. Being humble is an important part of feeling freedom inside, and the more we expand our awareness, the more we offer humility to our body and compassion to the world.

Difficulties bring some people to the spiritual path, but it doesn't matter. At some point, everyone feels the pain of a life situation; no one is exempt. The question is, How do we show

---

* To read more about the classes I teach in my home studio, visit www.mellara.com.

up to life? Having a daily practice, a time each day when we feel inner contentment, helps sustain us in difficult moments. Prayer, chanting, or meditation are not for everyone. For some, going for a walk, looking at beautiful art, or even cutting the grass can be a practice. Having a consistent practice is extremely helpful in keeping things from getting out of hand. We need to become aware of the delusions lurking behind the tall grasses of life.

Now when I sit quietly, I ask myself, "Who am I? Who is carrying this body?" The answer is not my identity, gender, or thoughts, but what I'm feeling and sensing inside. Sometimes I meditate on acceptance. I longed for my mum's acceptance, but she could never offer it; she was too wounded herself. Now, trusting my own inner voice, that my voice does matter, makes me a better parent and partner and perhaps a better daughter too, as I accept, forgive, and love my parents as they are. Through inquiries like these, I discover more and more about myself.

Once we see how our experiences have shaped us, we can recognize how our families, ancestors, life situations, and disappointments are our spiritual teachers. We somehow made the necessary adjustments and survived it all, like a great adventure. With wonder and gratitude, we can revisit these survival strategies and the possibility that we don't need them anymore. At that point, if we feel safe enough to venture beneath them, we can feel the actual brilliance underlying the strategy and the luminosity of who we really are.

I've moved my shrine from the spare room in our house to the yoga studio in our yard in order to share it with the beautiful souls who join me for living in awareness practice. I place fresh flowers on it, alongside statues of the Buddha, Mother Mary, Shiva, Kwan Yin, an elephant, and a porcelain apple tree that Channa gave me before I left Australia. I light a candle for all of my teachers past and present every morning, and sit quietly in the silence of the new day.

May we awaken from our daydreams, our nightmares, and being victimized by our thoughts, and instead witness them and experience liberation from within, moving toward the peace that has for a very long time been waiting for us to embody. In kindness, we put cruelty to ourselves and others to rest. In grace, we hold the horns of life. In humility, we soar into freedom. In generosity, we open our hearts to greater love. We all breathe the same air. We're all in this together. Freedom is possible; it's why we've been brought together. My teacher always encourages me to be all that the universe holds and never to separate from myself. The limitations I've felt in my life, and we all feel that sometimes, are pathways of mind, not who we really are. The infinite is beyond the knowing capacity of mind.

Channa always asks me to witness these states without being bound by them, and in fact to celebrate *beingness* at the same time. We are more than little blips living on earth; we have the power of the divine within us to transform suffering into joy and bring forth a profound healing. It was in this spirit that I dared write a book of my experiences, and I humbly offer it to you.

ACKNOWLEDGMENTS

Dear Mike, my beloved partner for life, father of our wonderful children, and best friend, thank you for not giving up on me, or us, and for always being my rock! You are my great protector, my knight in shining armor, and you make me laugh so hard. Thank you for the many gifts you bring our union; I'm grateful to walk alongside you. This is your book too, for without you I never would have felt the world to be safe enough to do what I'm meant to do. You make me feel supported and loved in a way no one else ever has.

Dear Leela, you're a bright shining star with the energy and light of all the stars in the universe! Thank you for your compassion that goes beyond your fourteen years. You love me unconditionally and you always seem to bring our family together in times that are challenging. You're a miracle. My dear friend and son, Charlie, you're the apple of my eye. You understand me deeply and love me as I am. You are kind, trustworthy, and an altogether great human being. Thank you for choosing me as your mother this time around! I am so grateful I get to do what I do. If it weren't for Mike and our kids holding my hand every step of the way, my dream of a studio, a steady practice of living in awareness, and now a book would not have been possible! And Rosie, our little muffin of a dog! Thank God Leela pushed so hard for you! Your devotion and selfless acts are an inspiration. I learn from you each and every moment.

Dear Papa, thank you for the years we had together. You did your best with me and our family, and in the end that's all any of us can do. And thank you for taking me out for ice cream as often as you did! Dear Mammiee, you have a heart of gold. Thank you for always allowing me to see the good in everyone. I remember your kindness, and thank you for believing in me. Dear Mum, you're a huge energy wrapped in creative greatness. Thank you for bringing me into this world. Things have been challenging between us, yet I know in my heart I was sent to you to learn the depths of love. Dear Dad, I love you no matter what, and I'm sorry that things didn't always work out for us. I wish only good things for you, the best life can offer. Peace and blessings to you always.

Dear Brother Jason, I'm sorry I left you so early. I guess that sometimes happens when you're the firstborn—leaving behind the siblings you yearn to love and spend more time with. When I left for America, there wasn't a day I didn't think of you. And now you've grown into such an incredible person. I am in awe of the way you and your beautiful partner Melanie take care of your gorgeous children. I am inspired by you both and love you more with every day.

My life changed the moment I heard Channa's name and saw a YouTube video of his magnificent sangha in Melbourne. I cherish every moment I spend with him, learning to live in awareness, and to be with myself thanks to his teaching and insight. I especially want to express my gratitude for his unconditional love and blessings. I am also deeply grateful to Darren Murphy, Channa's life partner, for sharing and taking such good care of this very special teacher. Darren opens his heart and the home he and Channa created together to the many beings who come through the door. Darren's wisdom goes beyond his years, even beyond this world, embodying grace in every moment. Darren says he feels like the luckiest person in the world. To be with them, to watch love flow naturally between them, is a wonder I'll always cherish.

Profound thanks to our newly formed East Bay Yoga community for all your kind thoughts, energy, and love, and especially to my dharma sister Suzy Dito, the yin to my yang, and the yang to my yin. I appreciate you so, and honor the gifts you bring to our friendship. Thank you for being you and for listening to me countless times when I would talk about what I was going through during the process of writing this book and beyond! You are a true friend, and you "see me," for which I am eternally grateful.

Sara Hoffa, from the moment we met I felt so connected to you, so comfortable to be with you. Through every change, marriage, or situation I found myself in, you provided a shoulder to cry on and gave me your futon when I had nowhere to go. You never once turned your back or judged me; you are a constant sunrise in my life. Thank you for the tremendous gifts you bring to my life. I can count on you no matter what, and I am beyond grateful.

Paulette Dwyer, I cherish our friendship and am honored to have shared in so many yoga adventures with you. You are always in my heart no matter where our souls may take us.

Elyse Lewin, you have always been my cheerleader and at every fork in the road you have given me sound advice that I have come to rely upon. You told me to never forget *Per aspera ad astra!* Through the rocks to the stars! Yes this is our motto! I adore and love you always.

Katie Mahon, you are a miracle! You stepped into my life at just the right time to help guide this manuscript along. Thank you for your generosity of spirit—you really do walk your talk!

Lisa Carta, you are not only an incredible artist but you are witty, fun, and poetic. Thank you for your grace, talent, and patience as we began to work so smoothly together flowing with the energy of this book. Your attention to detail and love is evident with this stunning cover.

Dear Arnie Kotler, I remember being in Bali for the November 2016 retreat and sending a prayer to the universe to please send me an editor who would be complementary to me. Suzy was with me when I made this wish. When I returned to the States, I started to look around on the internet and found you! I remember feeling vulnerable when we were first on the phone and you asked to see the manuscript. As it turned out, I was more than in good hands. Your artful questions and quiet direction encouraged me to discover ever more feelings, without feeling judged. You gave my book the flow it was yearning for and brought it to life!

You've been so loving and patient with this first-time writer, and I am grateful from the depths of my being.

Dear Jennifer Leigh Selig, thank you for you and for believing in me and this book! You see me as I am and for that I am grateful. I'm inspired by you and our connection to bring meaningful work into the world. I knew your company Mandorla Books was the right publisher the day I received my first email from you. You are generous and fierce in your truth-seeking question-asking, and for that I am eternally grateful. Today I understand that ALWL was not ready to be birthed until the right midwife came on board, and it was YOU! You have made a huge difference in my life and I have learned so much from you and our time together.

And last but not least, I thank you, dear reader, for staying with this long book all the way to the end! I hope my life's journey and the teachings of living in awareness that I discovered and continue to practice can help you, too, cultivate a life worth living.

Namaste,
Mellara Gold

GLOSSARY

asana: yoga pose to open the body.

Ayurveda: a system of medicine based on the premise that every person is made of five elements—space, air, fire, water, and earth—which combine to form three life forces, called doshas.

being: effortless flow.

beingness: non-doing presence.

Buddha-nature: true nature, being-nature, the fundamental capacity of all beings to awaken.

consciousness: awareness.

ego: everyday mind, self-identity.

elements (five): see entry for *ayurveda*.

guides: spirit beings that assist in life's journey.

higher consciousness: immersion in transcendence.

intellect: problem-solving capacity of the mind.

intuition: understanding viscerally, without need for reason; also *intuitive intelligence.*

mantra: a sound repeated to help us connect with ourselves and to a deeper reality.

mind: a set of cognitive faculties including consciousness, imagination, perception, thinking, judgment, language, and memory. The term *mind* is usually used in living in awareness practice to mean out-of-control small mind.

nirvana: transcendent state in which greed, hatred, and delusion have been extinguished and suffering has ceased.

no self: the Buddha's teaching that there is no permanent, autonomous self.

path: journey toward realization which is unique to every individual.

persona: from the Latin meaning "character mask"; the image we present for others to perceive.

practice: meditation, yoga, or engaging the teachings in everyday life.

prana: life force, energy.

puja: a ritual in which meditational prayers are offered to holy beings to request their blessings or help.

samadhi: state of concentration in which only witnessing and space remain.

satsang: a group of spiritual seekers gathered to be with a teacher.

soul: the spiritual or immaterial aspect of being.

thinking: using the mind to reflect, perseverate, or obsess about ideas of past or future.

unconditioned space: a pregnant presence in flow with the mystery of each moment as it is.

unconscious: not conscious.

witnessing: observing our own life neutrally, without affect; being present and noticing, not judging.

yoga: literally "union" of the individual with divine consciousness; spiritual discipline that includes breath control, meditation, and postures, widely practiced for health and wellness.

yoga nidra: state of consciousness between waking and sleeping; deep relaxation.

PRACTICES

❧

Sitting Meditation

Sit comfortably on the floor or upright on a chair with your feet planted firmly on the ground. If you're on the floor, place a blanket or a cushion beneath your sit bones so your hips are slightly higher than your knees. As you position yourself, move gently from side to side to see if any adjustments will make you feel more at ease. You don't have to look like a picture-perfect meditator; just sit in a way that feels comfortable.

If you can, relax your face, your jaw, your eyes, your forehead, and the space between your eyes slowly, one by one. Whatever comes up in your body, emotions, or thoughts, simply witness it. There might be tightness in areas you're just beginning to notice or a mind busy with thoughts. Whatever arises, allow each thing to be as it is. If there are sounds like birds chirping outside or smells like someone preparing a meal, open yourself up to it all. As you are able, enter into unconditioned, nonjudgmental space where you are open to the energy of this moment.

If your palms are facing up, it might mean that your body is being called to expand. If your palms are facing downward on your knees, you might be intuitively feeling the need for grounding. Either way is okay; simply observe your body's intelligence. Sit in this way for a few moments—sensing, discovering, and allowing what is. Be with your natural breathing. Be *in* your body. Feel the connection to your heart center.

See, also, the instructions on pages 169-172.

Ujjayi Breathing

Take a few deep breaths in through your nose and out through your mouth. Now bring your hands or a hand up to your face like a mirror right in front of your nose and your mouth, and take a deep breath in through your nose and exhale through your mouth, fogging up the pretend mirror in front of you. Now do it again. Can you hear the sound you are making as the mirror fogs up?—"ahhhh," almost like Darth Vader. Do this one more time.

Then take another deep in-breath, and as you're beginning to fog up the mirror, close your mouth while continuing to fog up the mirror, this time with your mouth closed. Inhale again, then exhale the same way, fogging up the mirror with your mouth closed. Continue the same way. This is ujjayi breathing.

You're putting a slight constriction in the back of the throat or the larynx (voice box, at the top of the throat), allowing the breath to pass through a thin space. And when it does, it creates this audible sound, just enough that you can hear it, perhaps reminding you of the ocean or listening to a sea shell by your ear, but not so loud that someone five feet away can hear you, allowing it to be gentle. Continue practicing for 2–5 minutes, or more if you'd like.

Continue expanding your lungs, feeling the breath as it gently flows in and out of your body, breathing this way throughout your sitting meditation or while practicing any yoga stretches you feel called to do.

This type of breath is not recommended while you're on a cardio machine, walking really fast, or bike riding. It's for yoga or meditation practice. Ujjayi breathing generates heat in the body, purifying the body from the inside out. Hearing the ocean-like sound is a wonderful reminder that we're breathing, connecting body, heart, and mind. Yoga means "union," after all.

Alternate-Nostril Breathing

Place your left hand facing either up or down on your thigh, close to your knee or on your lap, whatever feels most comfortable.

Use your right thumb to block off the right side of your right nostril. Then exhale from your crown and down through the left nostril, and continue down the left side of your spine. If possible, take a slight pause at the bottom of the exhale before inhaling up the left side, keeping the thumb on the right nostril. Hold your breath for a moment at the top of the inhale by pinching your nose, using your ring finger to help you.

Then exhale again down the right side of your spine, keeping your ring finger on the left nostril. If you can, visualize each vertebra as your breath travels slowly down and exits your body and into the earth. Take a short pause, if possible, before inhaling up the right side, taking your time to feel the fullness of your breath and your attention as it goes past the third eye (middle of the forehead) and out through the crown. Then pinch your nose and hold your breath for a moment.

After that, exhale all the way down the left side (keeping your thumb on the right nostril), again pausing for a moment before inhaling up through the left side. Repeat this as many times as it feels right for you, up to 5-10 rounds.

Build up to pausing—holding the breath—at the top of the inhale and at the bottom of the exhale. If you're pregnant, avoid holding your breath.

If it feels right for you to try, sit for a few moments after these breathing exercises and gently observe your body, noticing if there have been any shifts or changes.

ABOUT THE AUTHOR

Mellara Gold is a teacher of yoga and meditation based in Northern California. She was born in Queensland, Australia, and at the age of seventeen moved to Los Angeles to attend the prestigious Lee Strasberg Theatre Institute. After roles in *Don't Look Back* with Peter Fonda (1996), and *Love Boat: The Next Wave* (1998), a depleting injury led her to embark on a healing journey. At the Center for Yoga and other LA studios, she immersed herself in Hatha, Iyengar, Viniyoga, Ashtanga, and other types of yoga. Her first teacher training was at the Center for Yoga, and later she trained with Erich Schiffmann and Saul David Raye.

In 2015, after teaching yoga for eighteen years, Mellara studied at the Dassanayaka Yoga Centre in Melbourne, Australia, under the guidance of Sri Lankan yoga master, healer, intuitive, monastically-trained Buddhist upāsaka, chef, and founder of Uniting Awareness practice, Channa Dassanayaka. In 2017, after returning back to the Bay Area where she lives with her husband and two children, she leads workshops, retreats, and trainings (see https://mellara.com/). She is a regular contributor to *Elephant Journal* and other lifestyle and spiritual platforms. (Photo by In Her Image Photography)

Made in the USA
Las Vegas, NV
20 December 2021

38927235R00144